MW01070750

Stonington's
STEAMBOAT HOTEL

Stonington's

STEAMBOAT HOTEL

STUART VYSE

THE
History
PRESS

Published by The History Press
Charleston, SC
www.historypress.com

Copyright © 2022 by Stuart Vyse
All rights reserved

Front cover: Photos courtesy of the Stonington Historical Society. *Back cover*: Map courtesy of the Stonington Historical Society. Photo courtesy of the author.

First published 2022

Manufactured in the United States

ISBN 9781467152952

Library of Congress Control Number: 2022939484

Notice: The information in this book is true and complete to the best of our knowledge. It is offered without guarantee on the part of the author or The History Press. The author and The History Press disclaim all liability in connection with the use of this book.

All rights reserved. No part of this book may be reproduced or transmitted in any form whatsoever without prior written permission from the publisher except in the case of brief quotations embodied in critical articles and reviews.

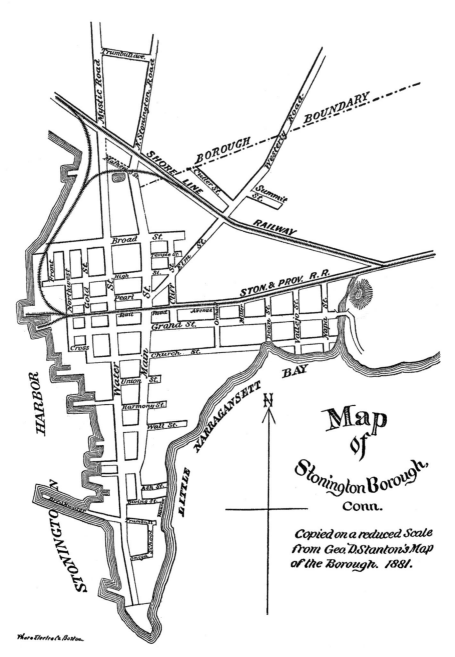

A simplified version of the 1881 map of Stonington Borough that appeared in the town directory that year. *Courtesy of the Stonington Historical Society.*

In memory of
Anthony Bailey and Jack Fix

The Steamboat Hotel is still standing, and we trust it will continue to do so for years without number.

—Stonington Mirror and Mystic Journal, *January 8, 1937*

CONTENTS

The Harbor View Apartments (formerly the Steamboat Hotel) as the building appears today. Pearl Street is on the left, and the building faces Gold Street and the town docks. *Author photo.*

PROLOGUE

In August 1999, during Blessing of the Fleet weekend, I moved to the Harbor View Apartments at 23 Gold Street, Stonington, Connecticut, and soon after, I met Margarethe "M." Thomas, a local real estate agent and longtime Stonington resident, at the Stonington Farmer's Market. M. had an apartment in the Seidner Block, also on Gold Street, and she asked me where I lived. In those days, the farmer's market was held next to the playground at the town docks, so I simply pointed to my building. She said, "Oh, you live in the Heartbreak Hotel." It is unclear who first gave the building that name, but several sources in town say it goes back to the 1960s or '70s. I was newly divorced at the time, so the name seemed fitting. From that day forward, whenever someone in town asked me where I lived, I said "at the Heartbreak Hotel." Because the real name of the building is not well known, I believe most people still know it by the name M. Thomas passed down to me. I have not tested the theory, but I believe that a piece of mail addressed to "The Heartbreak Hotel, Stonington, CT 06378" would find its way to the right place.

Much later, I learned that the building had actually been a hotel at one time, the Steamboat Hotel, and that it was very old. In 2020, when the coronavirus pandemic arrived, I stumbled across a few notable events that had happened at the Steamboat Hotel and became interested in the history of the building, eventually committing to this project. It is perhaps a romantic notion, but I believe that if you look deeply enough into any topic, you will eventually find something interesting. This belief may say more about the virtues of a curious mind than any object of study, but in this case, I had the advantage that the Steamboat Hotel was a hotel.

One of the defining features of homelessness is the absence of privacy. Those of us with places to live have the ability to keep out of public view those things we'd rather not display. Having spaces we can control allows us to regulate who knows about the happenings in our rooms, and a hotel room is a temporary place of privacy for the person who has rented it. Perhaps it is this mixture of public and private that has fascinated the many writers who've used hotels as the settings for novels and films.

The privacy of hotel rooms presents a barrier to the prying eyes of the historian, but in addition to offering beds to the itinerant public, over its history, the Steamboat Hotel housed several small businesses, including saloons, restaurants, a tobacco shop, a pool hall, a barbershop and a tailor shop, and some of the people who spent time there became important figures in the Borough of Stonington and far beyond. After two years of research, the building had not revealed all its mysteries, but I'd uncovered a story that adds to the history of the Borough of Stonington and of America in the nineteenth and early twentieth centuries. This book is the result of that effort.

Part of the appeal of this project was the opportunity to highlight people from the past who had gone largely unmentioned in previous accounts. With a few exceptions, the people of this story are not war heroes, statesmen or town fathers. Because the inspiration for this effort was a working hotel, saloon and boardinghouse, most of the people you will meet were members of an emerging nineteenth-century merchant class made possible by industrialization and advances in transportation. At its core, this is a story about small retail entrepreneurs and service workers, people who made their livings serving the public. Many were European immigrants or first-generation Americans who, for reasons of their own, settled on a tiny peninsula in southeastern Connecticut. The census data and other information that is available reveals a nineteenth and early twentieth century Stonington that was far more diverse than it is today. The borough was home to native Americans, free Blacks, "mulattos," Jews and Christians, as well as immigrants from England, Germany, Austria, Russia, Scotland and Ireland. The people of the Steamboat Hotel did not keep their letters and donate them to university libraries upon their deaths. I have pieced together the outlines of their lives from public records, newspaper accounts and the few written histories that have been preserved by local historical associations.

As a result, this book represents the only written biography for many of the people you will meet in the following pages.

Because there are gaps and unanswered questions in this story, I often had the urge to become a novelist and impose a coherent plot, but in general, I have avoided this temptation. Even under circumstances of more complete information, we are often opaque to each other and ourselves. In this account, I occasionally speculate about possible explanations for the twists and turns of the plot, but in an effort to do justice to the real people who produced this story, in most cases, I've left the unanswered questions unanswered.

SV
The Heartbreak Hotel
Stonington, CT

CHAPTER 1

STONINGTON STEAM

I n the middle of the nineteenth century, the little borough of Stonington, Connecticut, was profoundly changed by the arrival of steam power from both land and sea. The inexorable progress of invention and several accidents of geography brought the world to a tiny seaside village and, among other things, made the Steamboat Hotel possible.

THE FIRST EFFORTS TO develop a steam-powered boat began in the late 1700s but did not produce a commercially successful vessel until 1807, when Robert Fulton brought a steam engine built by Scottish inventor James Watt to New York and installed it in the *North River Steamboat*, which later became popularly known as the *Clermont*.[1] During the War of 1812, the British naval blockade of the eastern seaboard delayed the expansion of steamboat travel in the northeast, but by 1816, steam-powered boats began following the southern New England coast, traveling between New York City and ports in Connecticut and Rhode Island. Long Island Sound provided a protected waterway from New York City to Rhode Island, but travel to Boston was blocked by Cape Cod, which would not be bisected by a canal until 1916. In addition, the long trip around the Cape went through open seas that required steamships built for that environment. As a result, throughout the nineteenth century, the journey from New York to Boston usually meant a mix of sea and land travel. Steamboats would often dock at Providence, Rhode Island, and travelers would continue north by stagecoach. Soon, however, land-based steam power emerged to fill the gaps.

By the 1830s, iron rails began to etch the New England countryside. Transportation by rail, trolley and, eventually, automobile would ultimately replace the steamboats altogether, but in addition to moving freight from place to place, an important goal of early railroad expansion was to connect with steamboat lines at points where land transportation was required. In 1831, the Boston & Providence railroad was chartered to connect those cities, making it possible to travel from New York to Providence by steamer and continue on to Boston by train.[2]

The protected waters of Long Island Sound provided a relatively smooth ride, but at the eastern end of Long Island, vessels bound for Providence had to pass through the rough open waters off Point Judith, Rhode Island, before turning north into Narragansett Bay. As a result, as soon as the Boston to Providence railroad was completed, plans were made to extend the line to Stonington, Connecticut, the easternmost port that was still within the shelter of Long Island Sound. The geography of the Connecticut coastline prevented the introduction of direct rail travel from Providence to New York for several decades until railroad bridges could be constructed across the Thames River at New London and the Connecticut River at Old Saybrook. Until the completion of the train bridge over the Thames River in 1889, the best way to travel between Boston and New York in the mid-nineteenth century was by steamboat connecting with a steam train. The port at Stonington offered a calm passage through Long Island Sound, followed by rail transport to Providence and Boston.

Providence was the first city to offer direct steamboat service to New York, beginning in 1822. During this early period of steam-powered travel, the industrialist Cornelius Vanderbilt invested heavily in steamboats, hoping to establish a monopoly in the New York to Boston corridor, but by 1850, he'd liquidated all his steamboat interests in order to concentrate on westward railroad development.[3]

In 1833, the New York, Providence and Boston Railroad hired Whistler's father—the great railroad engineer Major George Washington Whistler, whose son would become the famous painter James Abbott McNeill Whistler—to design a line between Providence and Stonington.[4] Unfortunately, neither the people nor the geography of Rhode Island proved welcoming to the laying of what was called the "Stonington Road." In East Greenwich, Rhode Island, the tracks went through a farmer's peach orchard, and he scared off the workers with shotgun fire and threw their tools in the water. In addition, there was opposition to the road by citizens of both Wickford and Kingston Hill, so the engineers plotted a new course

An advertisement for the Providence and Stonington Steam Ship Company from the 1875 *ABC Pathfinder Railroad Guide*, "Avoiding Point Judith" and highlighting the "inside route via Providence and Stonington."

along the shore in East Greenwich that avoided the peach orchard and then turned inland, keeping its distance from both Wickford and Kingston Hill. But that was not the end of the difficulties.

As they brought the tracks south near Kingston, Rhode Island, the engineers encountered Rhode Island's Great Swamp, which extended almost to the town of Westerly on the state border. Railroad tracks are traditionally laid on crushed stone ballast to provide stability, and according to legend, as the tracks were built across the swamp, ballast had to be dropped down over seventy feet underwater to create a solid foundation.[5]

The six miles of track from the Rhode Island border to Stonington Borough were the first in the state of Connecticut, and in 1937, the road was finally completed, its rails cutting through the heart of the borough, across Main and Water Streets, extending onto what is now the town docks.[6] Suddenly, the quiet borough of Stonington had become an important transportation hub.

A November 20, 1895 photo taken from the clocktower of the Congregational church on Main Street in Stonington Borough looking west down Pearl Street toward the steamboat landing and train depot. The roof and third floor of the Steamboat Hotel can be seen just below the steamboat in the center. Most of the buildings in the foreground are still standing, with the notable exception of the Baptist church at the right. The Potter Block, which today is only two stories tall rather than three, can be seen just to the left of the church across Water Street, which runs right and left in the photo (north and south). The Müller Block is behind the Potter Block. Left of center, the railroad tracks run west through town to the steamboat landing. *Courtesy of the Stonington Historical Society.*

WHEN THE STONINGTON LINE was completed, Major Whistler moved to the borough, because it became clear the railroad would require an engineer's continuing attention.[7] During his time there, Whistler became very attached to Stonington and often said he wanted to make it his final home. For a time, he consulted on the construction of the Western Railroad of Massachusetts, but in 1842, he accepted the invitation of Emperor Nicholas I to build the railroad between Moscow and St. Petersburg, Russia. Whistler's family remained behind, living in Captain Amos Palmer's house at the corner of Main and Wall Streets.[8] Whistler died in St. Petersburg in 1849, but his body was transported to Boston and then finally to the Stonington Cemetery for burial. Two of his children had died while still very young and were buried in the cemetery in Stonington: Joseph Swift Whistler (1825–1840) and Kirk Boott Whistler (1838–1842). Their father had expressed the desire to be buried with them.[9] One author described the small ceremony at his interment this way:

> *A deputation of engineers, who had been in their early years associated with him, attended the simple service which was held over his grave and all felt, as they turned away, that they had bid farewell to such a man as the world has not often seen.*[10]

On the sunny morning of November 10, 1837, the newly launched steamboat *Narragansett* arrived in Stonington harbor to the sound of ceremonial cannon fire—perhaps from the same guns that now reside in Cannon Square in the borough and that prevailed valiantly against the British in the famous Battle of Stonington in 1814. On board were the president and board of directors of the newly formed Stonington Steamship Line, as well as approximately one hundred passengers who had left New York City the evening before. Upon arriving at the pier, the travelers were greeted by a cheering crowd of townspeople. This was just the beginning of a long day of festivities.[11]

The passengers formed a procession and, accompanied by the boat's brass band, marched up to the newly constructed Wadawanuck Hotel,

An 1849 sketch of George Washington Whistler's grave site in Stonington by his son James McNeill Whistler. *Library of Congress.*

which stood where the Stonington Free Library stands today, in what is now Wadawanuck Square. There they were treated to an elaborate breakfast before returning to the pier, where they boarded two trains festooned with American flags that took them off to Providence for lunch. In Providence, the New Yorkers were joined by contingents from Providence and Boston before everyone boarded the return train to Stonington. Back up at the Wadawanuck Hotel, an even more elaborate dinner was served for almost four hundred people. The governor of Connecticut and the mayor of Providence were both in attendance, and over thirty toasts were offered, including one to Major George Washington Whistler. At eleven o'clock, the whistle of the *Narragansett* blew, and the crowd proceeded to the pier, where the New Yorkers boarded the *Narragansett* and the Providence and Boston groups boarded the trains. Finally, steam engines took all the visitors away, leaving the local residents alone again. But Stonington Borough would never be the same.

CHAPTER 2

STONINGTON HOTELS OF THE STEAM ERA

It is hard to imagine how dramatically Stonington Borough changed with the arrival of steamboats and railroad cars. Beginning in the mid-seventeenth century, Stonington had a brisk whaling and seal industry that only ended after the Civil War.[12] Whales were hunted for oil, whale bone and "sperm" (ambergris), which was used in the manufacture of perfume. Seals were hunted for their furs. Stonington's sailing ships traveled the globe in search of these animals, and in the southern hemisphere summer of 1820–21, Stonington's most famous ship captain and seal hunter, Nathaniel B. Palmer, sailed the sloop *Hero* to the Antarctica peninsula and discovered an area now known as Palmer Land. During the peak years of these nautical industries, Stonington Borough was a prosperous and busy place, but the arrival of smoky, chugging steamboats and locomotives created new challenges for the local residents.

When the plushly furnished cars of the Boston, Providence and Stonington Railroad left the pier to take those first New York dignitaries to Providence on November 10, 1837, they were pulled by teams of horses for the first part of the trip. The borough elders had banned the use of locomotives, and as a result, trains were pulled by straining horses until they crossed Orchard Street on the east side of town, at which point steam engines were attached for the rest of the journey to Providence. But this nod to civility did not last long. The ordinance preventing engines in the borough was soon reversed, and the railroad built a car house and a roundhouse for engines on the west side near the steamboat pier. The effect of this invasion of iron beasts was profound.

G 3281 Steamboat Landing, Stonington, Conn.

I hope to see you soon, With love,
Louisa.

A steamboat at the Stonington steamboat landing. The photo is taken looking northwest across the southern pier (covered with railroad tracks). The steamboat is docked on the southern side of the northern pier, next to the train depot. *Author's collection.*

DURING THE NINETEENTH CENTURY, most of the passenger steamboats on Long Island Sound were night boats. Whether you were going east to Boston or west to New York, you would begin your journey in the early evening and arrive at your destination the next morning. For example, people traveling to Boston or Providence on the Stonington Line would report to the pier on the Hudson River side of lower Manhattan at 6:00 p.m., and as the steamer made its way south around the tip of Manhattan, back north into the East River, through Hell's Gate and east into Long Island Sound, passengers would be free to eat dinner in the dining room. Many of the night boats had ornately decorated saloons and music provided by a live band. Once passengers grew weary, cabin berths were available for all travelers, and individual state rooms could be reserved for an additional fee. The steamer would arrive at Stonington at approximately 4:20 a.m., at which point passengers and freight were loaded onto waiting railroad cars headed north, arriving at the end of the line in Boston in the vicinity of 7:00 a.m.

Westward travel was similar. Passengers would board a train in Boston at 5:00 or 6:00 p.m., arriving at the depot on the pier in Stonington approximately two and a half hours later. After transferring to a steamer,

STEAMER NEW HAMPSHIRE.
Menu.

Blue Points on half shell............ 25

SOUPS

Consomme............ 20	Julienne............ 20
Chicken............ 20	Puree of Tomato............ 20
Bisque of Clam............ 20	Mock Turtle............ 25

FISH

Pan Fish............ 25	Mackerel, Salt............ 35
Bluefish, broiled............ 40	Cod, fried fresh............ 25
Smelts, fried or broiled............ 40	" Fish Balls............ 25
" with tartar sauce............ 50	Bacon Garniture, with Fish extra.... 15

SHELL FISH

Oysters, stewed............ 25	Oyster Fritters............ 35
" Boston stew............ 35	Crabs, Soft Shell............ 50
" broiled............ 35	Clams, stewed............ 25
" broiled with French Peas... 45	" fried............ 30
" Pan Roast............ 35	" Fritters............ 30
" fried in batter............ 35	" a la Newburg............ 75
" fried in crumbs............ 30	" Cocktail............ 25
" Cocktail............ 25	Lobster, Broiled, Live............ 75
Scallops, plain, fried............ 35	" a la Newburg............ 75
Lobster, Plain............ 40	

SALADS AND RELISHES

Lettuce, plain............ 20	Mayonnaise............ 10
" with Mayonnaise or French	Queen Olives............ 15
Dressing............ 30	Pickles............ 10
Salad, Lobster............ 50	Chow Chow............ 10
Salad, Chicken............ 50	Sardines............ 25
Salad, Lettuce and Tomato............ 30	Celery............ 20

TO ORDER

Steak, Beef, small............ 40	Chicken, Spring, broiled (half)....... 50
" Sirloin............ 60	" " fried (half)............ 50
" with Onions............ 75	Ham or Bacon, broiled............ 30
" with Tomato Sauce... 75	" " and Eggs broiled or fried 40
" with Mushrooms.... 85	Mutton Chops............ 35
" extra............ 90	" " Breaded, with Tomato
" with Onions.... 1.10	Sauce............ 50
" with Mushrooms 1.15	Pork Chops... 35
" Tenderloin............ 60	Veal Cutlet, plain or breaded.... 40
" with Tomato sauce 75	" breaded, with Tomato Sauce 50
" with Mushrooms.. 85	Tripe, fresh broiled............ 30
" with Onions.... 75	Calf's Liver and Bacon............ 35
" Porterhouse............ 1.25	Welsh Rarebit............ 35
" with Mushrooms 1.50	Golden Buck............ 40
" extra............ 1.75	Country Sausage............ 35
" with Mushrooms 2.00	Corned Beef Hash Browned............ 25
Steak, Hamburg............ 50	" " with Poached Egg 30

VEGETABLES

Potatoes, with Cream............ 15	Sweet Potatoes, fried............ 15
" Stewed............ 15	Sweet Potatoes, Grilled............ 15
" Hashed Brown............ 15	Peas, French............ 25
" French Fried............ 15	" Early June............ 15
" Lyonnaise............ 15	Corn, stewed............ 15
" Saute............ 15	Onions, fried............ 20
" Grilled............ 15	" boiled............ 15
" Saratoga............ 15	Rice, boiled............ 10
" Julienne............ 20	Tomatoes, stewed............ 15

COLD DISHES

Beef, Roast............ 45	Sandwich, Ham............ 10
Beef, Corned............ 25	" Sardine............ 25
Tongue, Beef............ 35	" Tongue............ 15
Ham............ 30	" Chicken............ 20
Sandwich, Club............ 25	" Cheese............ 10

FRITTERS

Peach Fritters............ 25	Banana Fritters............ 25
	Orange Fritters............ 25	

EGGS

Boiled or Fried, two............ 20	Omelet, with Ham............ 35
Poached, on Toast, two............ 25	" with Oysters............ 35
Scrambled, two............ 25	" with Tomatoes............ 40
Shirred, two............ 30	" with Mushrooms............ 40
Omelet, Plain............ 25	" with French Peas............ 40
" with Parsley............ 30	" with Kidneys............ 40

BREAD, ETC

Toast, Milk............ 15	Bread, Vienna............ 10
" Dry............ 10	" and Butter, plain............ 10
" Brown Bread............ 15	" Boston Brown............ 10
" Buttered............ 15	" Graham............ 10
" Cream............ 20	" Corn............ 10
Oatmeal, with Milk............ 15	Wafers, Soda............ 10
" " Cream............ 20	Rolls, French............ 10
Hominy, with Milk............ 15	Biscuit............ 10
" " Cream............ 20	" Pilot............ 10
Rice, with Milk............ 15	" Bent's Water............ 10
" " Cream............ 20	Griddle Cakes with Maple Syrup... 15
	Waffles............ 25

TEA AND COFFEE

Tea, cup............ 10	Tea or Coffee with Rolls............ 20
" Oolong, pot............ 15	Coffee, cup............ 10
" Green, pot............ 15	" pot............ 15
" English Breakfast, pot......... 15	Chocolate, pot............ 20
	Milk, per glass............ 05	

DESSERT

Pie, Peach............ 10	Pound Cake............ 15
" Apple............ 10	Sponge " 10
" Lemon............ 10	Ice Cream............ 15
Oranges, two............ 15	Bananas, two............ 10
" sliced, two............ 15	Prunes, stewed............ 10
Preserved Jinger............ 20	Currant Jelly............ 15
	Preserved Peaches............ 20	

CHEESE

American Cheese............ 10	Jar Admiral Cheese............ 20

HOURS FOR MEALS

Eastward.—*Dinner from* 6.00 P. M. *to* 9.00 P. M.   *Hot Coffee and Lunch from*
   3.00 A. M. until 6.00 A. M.   *Breakfast from* 6.00 A. M. *to* 8.30 A. M.
Westward.—*Dinner from* 6.00 P. M. *to* 7.30 P. M. *and from* 9.00 *to* 11.00 P. M.
   Hot Coffee at 5.30 A. M.   *Breakfast from* 6.00 A. M. *to* 8.30 A. M.

Passengers will please write their orders in full and note extension and addition of checks. Reasonable time should be allowed for cooking. Please summon the Steward if service proves unsatisfactory.

50-10-9-1901.

A 1900 menu from the Stonington Line boat *New Hampshire*. The menu also offered an extensive wine list. *Rare Book Division, New York Public Library.*

travelers would dine and be entertained as they made their slow progress through Long Island sound to New York, arriving at the Hudson River pier early the next morning.

The effect of this timetable on the Borough of Stonington was that most of the daytime hours were relatively quiet, but it was hard to get any sleep at night. Henry R. Palmer described the atmosphere this way:

> *Each evening, shortly after seven, the night crews would begin the steady shuttling of freight cars from the junction over the crossings and onto the sidings leading to the boats. The screaming of wheel flanges against curves and switches, the signaling toots of the locomotives, the clashing of car couplers and the clanking, rumbling of heavy drags getting under way went on most of the evening, interrupted only by arrival of the boat train from Providence. With the departure of the steamer amid a blowing off of steam and sounding of the siren and the deep throated whistle, activity in the yard would quiet down and remain quiet until the New York boat arrived. And*

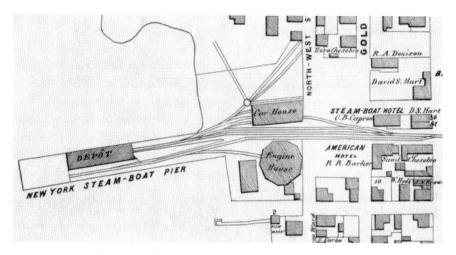

A detail from an 1851 map of Stonington Borough showing the "STEAM-BOAT HOTEL (C. B. Capron)" and, just below it, the "AMERICAN HOTEL (R. R. Barker)." The map also shows the web of railroad tracks that covered the west side of the borough. *Courtesy of the Stonington Historical Society.*

> *then pandemonium would once more break loose, as the unloading and reshuffling of cars commenced again, continuing on until daybreak. The Borough was not a peaceful place at night.*[13]

Because the streets going north and south were so closely spaced, a single train rolling through the borough could block traffic on two or three streets at once. The residents soon regretted their decision to allow locomotives in town and complained bitterly about the noise and inconvenience. Except for those businesses directly tied to steamboats and the railroad, the economy suffered, but nothing was done.

THE STEAMBOAT HOTEL

The Wheeler family of Stonington was so expansive that Richard Anson Wheeler's *History of the Town of Stonington* (published in 1900) lists 552 Wheelers born by the year 1851.[14] Number 406 was Gilbert Wheeler, the sixth child of Jonathan and Martha Stanton Wheeler, born on July 25, 1799. What little is known of Gilbert Wheeler suggests he was spirited, clever, successful, and prolific. According to an account by local historian Emma Palmer, as a young man, Gilbert played the bass drum with the Eighth Infantry Company of the Thirtieth Regiment of the Connecticut militia under the command of Captain Francis Amy, who, according to Palmer, was quite proud of his position as captain. William Potter had been the previous captain of the Eighth Infantry, during the British attack of 1814, but by this time, he was living in a house on Main Street in the block between Harmony and Wall Streets. In addition to being a veteran of the Battle of Stonington, Potter would go on to be the first keeper of the borough's first lighthouse at Stonington Point, but the more important fact for our story is that Gilbert Wheeler was engaged to Captain Potter's daughter, Esther. On one of their training days, as the company marched past the Potter house, Wheeler spotted Esther in a window and, in an effort to express his affection, began to beat his drum with such vigor that he broke the drumhead, spoiling the music for the rest of the day. Captain Amy was not amused.[15]

Despite the embarrassment of the broken drum, Gilbert went on to marry Esther Ann Potter in February 1829. Their first child, Harriet Elizabeth, died in July 1830 at the age of eight months, but the couple went on to have four more children—one boy and three girls—all of whom lived to adulthood and eventually married. Esther died at the age of twenty-nine on October 10, 1837, and Wheeler married his second wife, Angelina Byron Wood, in March 1840. Gilbert and Angelina had three more children.

Gilbert Wheeler was a farmer whose home and fields were south of Elm Street, just outside the borough, but with the arrival of the railroad and steamship lines, he must have recognized a business opportunity in town. In December 1837, a month after the *Narragansett*'s first triumphant visit to Stonington Harbor, Wheeler purchased from the New York, Providence and Boston Railroad a small, unused piece of land next to the tracks for $500. The narrow plot was on the southeast corner of Pearl and Gold Streets, a short distance from the new train depot. The parcel was so close to the tracks that the deed included a disclaimer that the railroad would not be held responsible for "loss by fire communicated from the Locomotives of said Company in their passages to or from their Depot belonging to said Company and their Car houses."[16] The building Wheeler built at Pearl and Gold caught fire a number of times but has managed to prevail for almost two hundred years.

From the beginning, the Steamboat Hotel appears to have been primarily a residential establishment—essentially a large boardinghouse—and saloon. Travelers also stayed at the hotel, but in 1850, an astonishing total of twenty-seven people were living in this modest two-story building—most of them permanent residents. The Steamboat's first manager was Colonel Bowen Capron.[17] According to the 1850 U.S. Census, Capron's family lived in the

The Steamboat Hotel in 1885, looking east from the railroad yard back toward the hotel entrance on Gold Street. This is the only known photograph of the hotel in its original two-story form. Three years after this photo was taken, the hotel was raised one story, and a new first floor was added. *Courtesy of the Stonington Historical Society.*

hotel, and including his wife, Susan, and his married daughter, Dorcas, there were only five female residents. The bulk of the tenants were single men who worked for the railroad as engineers, brakemen, firemen, conductors and railroad managers. Many people traveled to and from the hotel by horseback or stagecoach, and as a result, a few of the 1850 occupants were "hostlers," or livery managers. Finally, some hotel staff lived in the building, including a bartender, a waiter and housekeepers. The rooms were hardly bigger than the beds the residents slept in, and meals were offered in the basement tavern. The entrance to the building on Gold Street had a Dutch door, and Mr. Capron often kept the top half open so that he could lean out and call to his friends as they passed.

THE HOTEL WADAWANUCK

Given all the noise and smoke on the west side of the borough, it made sense that the Steamboat Hotel would be home to the railroad workers who were making all that noise and smoke. It was never designed as a luxury facility, and as the festivities of November 10, 1837, suggest, the Wadawanuck Hotel, a short walk up from the pier, was the premier establishment in town. The Wadawanuck was built in 1837 by the New York, Providence and Boston Railroad for the use of its patrons. Previously, the railroad had built the Tockwotton House hotel near the steamboat landing in the Fox Point neighborhood of Providence. Initially open year-round and later in summers only, the Wadawanuck was as close as Stonington ever came to having a grand resort hotel. The railroad soon sold the hotel, and it changed hands many times in its relatively short history.

In its prime, the Wadawanuck was the focus of the summer scene in Stonington, and when dignitaries came to town, they usually stayed at the Wadawanuck. In 1840, President John Tyler visited and was greeted with

Advertisement for the Wadawanuck hotel from the 1881 *Anderson's Stonington Directory.* *Courtesy of the Stonington Historical Society.*

a welcoming speech at the hotel by the warden of the borough, George E. Palmer.[18] The president was taken to see the eighteen-pound cannons that held off the British in 1814 and the dilapidated arsenal where they were being kept. Tyler, sometimes called "Old Veto" due to his propensity to use that power, promised that, if Congress passed an appropriation to repair the arsenal, he would not veto it, but the funds never arrived.

In the years between 1847 and 1857, many couples were married at the Wadawanuck due to a peculiarity in the Rhode Island marriage laws. Quick marriages were impossible in Rhode Island because couples were required to "read out" in church for three successive Sundays in order to qualify for marriage.[19] To avoid this procedure, many a runaway couple came across the border to be married by a minister in the borough. Parents of the couple were often savvy to this practice and followed in hot pursuit. As a result, borough ministers offered quick ceremonies, and the hotel provided a fresh team of horses for a speedy getaway to New London or Norwich to file the marriage papers.[20] The Steamboat Hotel was also known for hosting these runaway weddings.

In 1857, the Wadawanuck was purchased by the Reverend Harvey A. Sackett of New York, who refashioned it as the Wadawanuck Young Ladies Institute. According to historian Minor Myers Jr., this was the first women's college established in the state, and it had a distinguished but very brief run.[21] Reverend Sackett devised the curriculum and, with his wife, Diantha Sackett, operated the school, taught courses and hired instructors. The subjects offered included English literature, French, German, history, mathematics and natural science, as well as painting and drawing. The organist at the Calvary church taught music. For reasons that are unclear, the institute closed in 1863, and the Sacketts moved on to Ingham University in Leroy, New York.

Ira Palmer purchased the Wadawanuck from the Sacketts and reopened it as a hotel to renewed success. In the summer season, the hotel was sometimes unable to meet visitors' demands for lodging. Cots were placed in the hallways of the building, and some vacationing families were forced to find accommodations in the homes of borough residents. In August 1870, 169 people dined at the hotel in a single evening, and between June 20 and August 14, 1873, the hotel accommodated over 1,200 guests. The post–Civil War era of the early 1870s was particularly successful for the Wadawanuck. Yachting had grown in popularity, and New York yachting clubs often stopped in Stonington Harbor on the way to Newport. As is still the case today, many local people owned sailboats, and for several

An undated photograph of the Wadawanuck Hotel. *Courtesy of the Stonington Historical Society.*

years, the borough hosted a regatta on the Fourth of July. In 1873, the *Stonington Mirror* reported that the Wadawanuck hosted a reception and "hop" for the Brooklyn Yacht Club.[22]

In the summer months, the Wadawanuck was a social and cultural center of the borough. Guests who ate in the hotel dining room where often joined by townspeople who had become summer friends, and on other occasions, visitors were invited into local homes. The steamboat companies arranged excursions to Watch Hill and Newport, and in August 1872, the *Stonington Mirror* reported that a group of "young masters and misses stopping at the Wadawanuck" gave a performance of "Cinderella, or The Glass Slipper" in the parlor of the hotel for guests and borough friends. The production was organized by Laura Phillips, an actor from the Globe Theater in Boston who was also a guest at the hotel.[23] Phillips was described by the *Mirror* as a "prominent actress," but contemporary reviews were not always kind. In December 1870, Phillips appeared in the play *Fernande* at the Boston Museum theater, and according to a writer at the *Season*, "Phillips played the role of Fernande and very nearly ruined the piece thereby, her hard, unsympathetic, self-conscious manner being just what is most unsuited to the part."[24] She got better marks later that winter for a performance in the comedy *Central*

Park, where she was said to be "intensely funny, if a little coarse."[25] But her mentions in the *Stonington Mirror* make it clear that Phillips's residence at the Wadawanuck Hotel was a welcome addition to the summer season. She was recruited to give a reading to the local book club.

In the 1870s, the Wadawanuck was not an option for tourists of modest means. In 1872, a woman from Scranton, Pennsylvania, on vacation with her young daughter became stranded in Stonington en route to Block Island and described her dilemma this way:

> *Stonington with her steamboats and railroads (centered there), her half dozen millionaires and scores of citizens worth $50,000 to $500,000 has but one hotel—a first class, fashionable summer resort, open but two or three months in the year, prices there-at are necessarily high. Not caring to go where silks and satins rustled and diamonds and paint and blushes and paste commingled, we looked elsewhere.*[26]

The traveler spent two nights at the Tremont House on Water Street, where she complained to the proprietor, Richard. R. Barker, about the quality of the room and the price. For his part, Barker—about whom we will learn more later—claimed that, were it not for his rum business, he would not be able to make a living. The traveler finally found suitable lodging in a private home.

The eventual demise of the Wadawanuck Hotel was caused by several factors. The borough lacked some features that would make it competitive with other resort destinations. At the time, there was no beach in the borough, and in the 1850s, the hotel constructed a floating bathhouse in the middle of the harbor that was approached by a long pier at the foot of Broad Street. It included dressing rooms around the perimeter, an open area in the middle and stairs leading down to the water. At high tide in the summer, townspeople would walk down to Broad Street, pay a small fee and go for a swim off this floating platform, but in the late 1860s, the bathhouse came off its moorings, drifted across the harbor and was eventually set on fire.[27]

In those days, the breakwater, off what is now the Stonington Commons development, was a much more inviting structure than it is today, and hotel guests would often sunbathe on the rocks. But eventually, this lost its appeal for visitors in search of sun and surf. For a time, vacationers would take day trips by steamboat to Watch Hill and Newport to swim and shop, but as the resort industry continued to grow and transportation options

Undated postcard photo of the Stonington breakwater, a popular sunbathing spot for summer visitors. Also known as a place for "spooning" couples. *Courtesy of the Stonington Historical Society.*

The Steamboat Hotel and, directly across the tracks, the building that earlier held the American House hotel. Between 1888 and 1897, when this photo was taken, the Steamboat Hotel was at its full three-story height, and the former American House was the private residence of August Müller and family. J. L. "Pop" Prouty was superintendent of transportation for the railroad. *Courtesy of the Stonington Historical Society.*

became more plentiful, many travelers fled to places where beaches, shops and restaurants were closer at hand.

In addition, the hotel suffered the effects of a growing late-nineteenth-century temperance movement in the borough, which was making it difficult to serve alcohol. Guests were also prevented from bringing in wine.[28] In 1886, the Wadawanuck did not open for the season, and the final blow came in 1889, when the railroad bridge over the Thames River at New London was completed, marking the beginning of the end of Stonington's era as a major transportation hub. For the first time, travelers could now go from Boston to New York entirely by rail—eliminating the need for steamboats. In 1893, local builder Frank Sylvia and his sons tore down the Wadawanuck Hotel and used the wood to repair thirty houses they owned in the borough and to build a new one on Grand Street.[29]

THE AMERICAN HOUSE HOTEL

The American House hotel was just across the railroad tracks from the Steamboat Hotel, and in some ways the two establishments competed, while in others they did not. The hotel was built by Samuel Chesebro in 1836–37, as the railroad was coming to town, and it was first operated by a Mr. Van Cott, who died in the tragic fire and sinking of the steamer *Lexington*, about which we will hear more later. The second keeper was Richard R. Barker, who ran the hotel until 1855.

The American House distinguished itself by offering fine food and entertainment. The building had a large ell running south along Gold Street, which, on the first floor, contained a dining room with a fireplace that Mr. Barker used to roast oysters for guests and a table capable of sitting over fifty people. Above this room was another large hall that was used for various entertainments and was home to a school for popular dance.[30]

The primary competition between these neighboring hotels involved horses. Before 1858, the only public transportation between Stonington and New London to the west was by small steamboat. As a result, both Capron and Barker kept teams of horses in nearby stables and offered transportation by stagecoach to New London, which involved riding to Groton and crossing the Thames River to New London by ferry. The hotels provided door-to-door service. Anyone wanting to go to New London the following day would leave notice at the hotel. In the morning, a stagecoach picked up the traveler at home, and on the return trip, the driver dropped them back at their door.

August Müller family standing in front of his furniture store, the former American House hotel building, on Gold, probably between 1867 and 1887. *Courtesy of the Stonington Historical Society.*

The rivalry between the neighboring hotels was so intense that the fare dropped to just five cents from Stonington to New London and ten cents to return. After the Stonington to Groton leg of the railroad opened in 1858, it was possible to travel to New London by rail. Before the train bridge across the Thames River was completed in 1889, train cars were placed on ferries at Groton to cross the river to New London, but despite this oddity, many travelers found train transportation preferable to stagecoach. As a result, the local hotels suffered substantial declines in stagecoach ridership, but by then, the American House had closed.

In 1867, the American House building was purchased by August Müller, an immigrant from Prussia who, as was common in the eighteenth and nineteenth centuries, offered the combined services of cabinetmaker and undertaker.[31] Across the state line in Westerly, Rhode Island, H.B. Gavitt provided the same services.[32] The former American House hotel contained a furniture factory and display room, and Müller's two businesses came together with the offer of caskets "on the most reasonable terms." In 1887, Müller built the large three-story "Müller Block," which still stands on the opposite side of the Steamboat Hotel, just across Pearl Street. August "Augie"

Top: August Müller display advertisement from the 1881 *Anderson's Stonington Directory*. *Courtesy of the Stonington Historical Society.*

Bottom: Detail from a 1900 photograph taken from the docks looking east toward town. In the background (*left to right*) are the Müller Block (large square building), the Steamboat Hotel and the former American House Hotel. *Courtesy of the Stonington Historical Society.*

Müller was a highly respected member of the community. He was an officer of the Second Congregational Church and president of the Ram Island Gun Club, and both the furniture and undertaker businesses he established continued for three generations, ending with his grandson, August Owen Müller, who died in 1974.

THERE WERE OTHER HOTELS and boardinghouses in the borough, many of them not far from the Steamboat Hotel. William Hyde operated the Eagle Hotel on the northwest corner of Water and Grand Streets, but it burned to the ground on August 15, 1862, and was replaced by a delicatessen. Although the Eagle Hotel fire was a total loss, the carved wooden eagle that adorned the building was saved and for a time was in the possession of the Neptune Engine Company of the Stonington Fire Department.

After August Müller took over the former American House building, Richard Barker moved to the Tremont House hotel, the three-story building that still stands on the northeast corner of Water and Church (across Church Street from Noah's Restaurant). In 1877, the business changed management, Mr. Barker moved on, and the hotel was renamed the Ocean House. Perhaps due to its location in the commercial section of Water Street, the Ocean House was frequented by traveling doctors and salespeople. According to the *Stonington Mirror*, in the late summer of 1878, Dr. J. Briggs & Co. was at the Ocean House offering treatments for corns, troubling bunions and other foot problems,[33] and in August 1891, the "scientific optician" R.D. Hill was in residence.[34]

The Cassedy House hotel was on the corner of Grand and Water Streets, in the building that now houses Grand & Water Antiques. We know very little about the Cassedy House, but it was in operation at least between 1911 and 1931. A May 1931 notice in the *Stonington Mirror* praised the wisteria vines on the east side of the Cassedy House, which were said to have "unusually large and beautiful" blossoms.[35]

In 1930 and 1931, the borough was visited by Johnny J. Woods, the "Human Fly." Human flies were an enduring daredevil phenomenon of American history. In the first half of the twentieth century, a number of men traveled the country scaling buildings barehanded—typically in ordinary street clothes—before amazed crowds. After achieving the summit, the flies would perform dangerous stunts and gymnastic feats to the delight—and horror—of the audience below. Jack Williams was one of the most famous human flies, renting himself out to companies and organizations for literal publicity stunts.

Above and opposite: The "Human Fly," Johnny Woods, climbing and doing a headstand on top of the San Antonio Light Building in San Antonio, Texas, on January 6, 1940. This climb was done to publicize his climb of the much larger Plaza Hotel in San Antonio later in the month. *San Antonio Light Collection/San Antonio Express-News/ZUMA Press.*

In the late 1910s, he scaled the Woolworth Building in New York City, City Hall in Oakland, California, and many other buildings.

Human flies were often steeplejacks or steelworkers and were among the daredevils who eventually found work doing stunts in the movie industry.[36] In July 1922, silent film star Harold Lloyd witnessed Bill Strothers, a steelworker and human fly, climb the Brockman Building on Seventh Street

Harold Lloyd in the 1923 silent film *Safety Last! Hal Roach Studios. Author's collection.*

in Los Angeles and immediately wanted to use a similar stunt in a movie. Producer Hal Roach put Bill Strothers under contract for Lloyd's next and most famous film, *Safety Last!*, which includes the iconic scene of Lloyd hanging from a large clock on the outside of a skyscraper with moving traffic below. Strothers performed many of the climbing stunts in *Safety Last!*, and Lloyd was swapped in for closeup shots in the safer environment of a set built on the roof of a building.

Human flies often did their tricks for charity. Jack Williams raised money for World War I Liberty bonds, and Johnny Woods also did many stunts for causes. In other cases, human fly performances were a popular method of advertising businesses or commercial products. Often, the climber would

The Müller Block on the northeast corner of Gold and Pearl Streets as it appears today. The office of a real estate builder is on the first floor, and there are apartments on the upper floors. *Author photo.*

stop halfway up the building to speak to the crowd about the product or cause he was promoting, after which he would continue his ascent. Typically, when a human fly was raising money for a charity, assistants would pass through the crowd asking for donations, and the proceeds were split with the performer.

After a highly publicized accident in New York killed Harry Young as he climbed a building—somewhat ironically, to publicize the movie *Safety Last!*—the city prohibited people from climbing the outsides of buildings, but the practice continued elsewhere and never completely died out. On May 26, 1977, two years after Philippe Petit did his high-wire walk between the twin towers of the World Trade Center, George Willig, a mountain climber from Queens, New York, who called himself the Human Fly, scaled the south tower of the World Trade Center.

Johnny Woods was a successful human fly who appeared all over the country, often drawing large crowds. In September 1930, one thousand people crowded into Central Square, New Britain, Connecticut, to see him mount the Neri Building, and in 1947, eight thousand people witnessed him climb the Murchison Building in Wilmington, North Carolina.[37] Woods often worked his wife into his act, carrying her around on the tops of buildings while he was blindfolded. He claimed to hold the record for climbing the Woolworth Building in New York City, mounting all sixty-three stories in two hours and forty-five minutes.

Although tall buildings have always been scarce in Stonington, in 1930, Woods scaled the three-story Cassedy House hotel, and in 1931, he climbed the Müller Block at Gold and Pearl Streets—two of the tallest buildings in town. The *Stonington Mirror* article promoting the July 10, 1931 appearance said that Woods would perform antics on the roof of the Müller building.[38] In 1947, Mr. Woods was living in New London, Connecticut, and he returned to the borough to climb the Müller Block on Sunday, May 4, at 2:30 p.m. and again on Monday, May 5, at 3:30 and 7:30 p.m.[39]

FROM THE MID-NINETEENTH CENTURY through the early twentieth century, when Stonington was a transportation hub and before automobile ownership had become widespread, there were several hotels within a three-block radius of each other in the northern section of the borough, but the Steamboat, Wadawanuck and American House hotels were most closely tied to the railroad and steamship industries. As a result, they are the most important to our story.

CHAPTER 3

A COLD JANUARY NIGHT*

Although it had been demonstrated that steamboats could safely pass through the waters around Point Judith on their way to Providence or Newport,[40] that area of the New England coast's lasting reputation for a rough ride was sufficient to support the popularity of travel through Stonington for several decades. Despite the smooth waters of the Stonington line, it had its share of accidents and calamities.

In the mid-1860s, the Stonington boats were operated by the Merchants' Steamship Company, and the firm suffered a number of losses. The *Commonwealth* burned in December 1865, and in 1866, the *Commodore* was grounded in a storm off Long Island and subsequently sank. In addition, the company's steamboat *Plymouth Rock* was grounded off Old Saybrook. It was successfully refloated but at great expense. There were no casualties in any of these mishaps, but collectively, they pushed Merchants' into bankruptcy and interrupted service from Stonington for two years. A more serious accident happened on June 11, 1880.[41]

When the Stonington line was reestablished in 1868, it acquired two side-wheel paddle steamers named *Narragansett* and *Stonington*. On the foggy evening of June 11, the eastbound *Narragansett*, coming from New York,

---

* As one might expect of a famous story that has been repeated many times, accounts of the Lexington disaster and especially of David Crowley's survival vary considerably based on the source. I have done my best to create an accurate narrative, and in the case of Crowley's ordeal, I have relied as much as possible on a letter written by him to Captain James State of Stonington just two months after the incident. The original of this letter, dated March 4, 1840, is held by the Stonington Historical Society.

A Currier and Ives print depicting the collision between the *Stonington* and *Narragansett* on June 11, 1880. *Library of Congress 2002697103.*

collided with its sibling, the westbound *Stonington*. Lit by oil lamps and built of wood, the *Narragansett* caught fire, and thirty lives were lost. The *Stonington* sustained damage to the bow but no casualties and made it home to the borough, later sailing to New York for repairs. The *Narragansett* was raised and repaired at Palmer's boatyard in Noank, Connecticut. Both vessels continued to serve the Stonington line for another thirteen years.[42]

Despite these accidents, by far the most serious tragedy to befall a Stonington steamship—one with several connections to the Steamboat Hotel—happened very early in the history of the line.

In 1835, Cornelius Vanderbilt commissioned the construction of the *Lexington*, which was designed for speed. Early trips from New York to Boston required twenty-five hours of steamboat travel from New York to Providence, the first port to receive travelers headed to Boston, followed by an eight-hour stagecoach ride from Providence to Boston. The stagecoaches had to stop every eight or nine miles to acquire fresh horses, and during this transition, travelers would typically pause, according to one author, to "quaff spiritous drinks."[43] Technological advances greatly reduced these times by substituting railroad transport for stagecoach travel and through the development of faster steamboats. In May 1829, the steamer *Benjamin Franklin* made it from New York to Providence in fifteen hours and fifteen minutes, a new record.

A few years later, the Boston and Providence Railroad would connect those two cities, greatly reducing the overall travel time.

Vanderbilt supervised the building of the *Lexington* in New York, with the hope that it would be strong and fast. In the early days of steamboat travel on Long Island Sound, races for bragging rights were common. When the Stonington line opened in 1837, Providence resented the competition, and the Atlantic Steamboat Company claimed their *John W. Richmond* was faster than the Stonington boats. To settle the matter, a New York to Providence race was proposed between Providence's *Richmond* and Stonington's *Narragansett*. Unfortunately for the Providence contingent, the *Narragansett* arrived at the finish line an hour before the hometown boat.[44]

At the time, the *Lexington* was part of the Stonington Steamship Line, and in the hope of restoring its pride, the Atlantic Steamboat Company offered Vanderbilt $60,000 to buy the *Lexington*, provided it could beat the *John W. Richmond* in a head-to-head race. The *Richmond* was under the command of Captain William H. Townsend, and the *Lexington* was helmed by Cornelius Vanderbilt's brother Jake Vanderbilt. By marshaling as much of the hotter-burning resinous wood he could find onboard the *Richmond* and by pushing the engines to the limit, Townsend managed to pass through the rocks at Hell Gate first. The *Richmond* had been tied to its pier for an hour before the *Lexington* appeared. It was generally believed that the *Lexington* was the faster boat but that Townsend's strategic racing was responsible for his success.[45]

By 1840, Vanderbilt had begun to liquidate his holdings on Long Island Sound to concentrate on westward railroad expansion. He'd sold the *Lexington*, but it was still in service to the Stonington line, now under the command of a new captain, George Child. At four o'clock on January 13, 1840, Captain Child and a crew of forty set out on a routine trip to Stonington with over one hundred passengers onboard. Although it was a very cold evening and there were ice floes in the sound, there was no particular cause for concern because the *Lexington* was famous for its icebreaking ability. As it turned out, the weather did not cause the tragedy that resulted, but it greatly increased the loss of life. Far more important factors in the disaster that followed were the *Lexington*'s recent conversion from wood to coal—a fuel that burned much hotter—and the steamboat's non-human cargo that evening: bales of cotton picked by enslaved people in the south, on their way to textile mills in the north.

About seven o'clock, when the Lexington was near Eatons Neck, Long Island, fire broke out onboard, starting in the wood casing surrounding the engine's smokestack and soon spreading to the cotton bales and other freight. The fire traveled so quickly that by the time it was discovered, there was little that could be done. Captain Child attempted to steer the boat toward the Long Island coast, but a tiller line running from the wheel back to the rudder snapped, and the vessel became unmanageable. When Captain Child reluctantly gave the order to abandon ship, the boat was still under power, and the lifeboats capsized as soon as they hit the frigid water. One crashed into the still-turning side wheel.

In all, 143 souls perished in the fire or in the icy waters of Long Island Sound on the evening of January 13, 1840, and only four survived, three of them crew members of the *Lexington*. All of those who escaped floated to safety, not in lifeboats but on bales of cotton. Captain Chester Hilliard of Norwich, the one passenger who survived, was near the pilothouse when he realized Captain Child had lost control of the boat, and he remembered the cotton bales. He ran through the smoke and flames to the freight deck and located a cotton bale that had not yet caught fire. With the help of a fellow passenger, he threw the bale overboard, and both Hilliard and the man who had helped him leapt into the water and scrambled onto the bale, which measured just three by four feet. Hilliard managed to grab a floating piece

Currier lithograph of the "awful conflagration" of the *Lexington*. *Library of Congress 94507226.*

of wood that he used to steer the bale away from ice and debris. Despite their best efforts to stay warm, his companion on the bale, Benjamin Cox of New York, froze to death during the night, but at eleven o'clock the next morning, someone on the sloop *Merchant* spied the frostbitten Hilliard floating on his cotton bale and lifted him to safety.

Later, Stephen Manchester, the *Lexington*'s pilot, also floating on a cotton bale, was picked up by the sloop, and a fireman, Charles B. Smith, who floated much of the night on a cotton bale before transferring to a large wooden guardrail, was also saved. The *Merchant* found Smith at two o'clock, three hours after Hilliard was rescued.

Second mate David Crowley provided the Lexington's most harrowing and famous story of survival. Like the others, Crowley rode to safety on a cotton bale. Early in the emergency, he participated in the bucket brigade in an effort to douse the flames, and he was present when, with great sadness, Captain Child gave the order to abandon ship. Crowley leapt into the water with a wooden sideboard he hoped to ride, but when a cotton bale floated by, he climbed aboard. He floated on the bale without a coat or hat, and because no pieces of wood came within range, he just drifted, unable to steer or paddle. One of the ropes securing the bale had broken, and Crowley was able to dig out some of the cotton to form a hole for his legs. He stuffed the cotton he removed from the hole into his clothes to insulate himself against the cold.[46] The next morning, Crowley saw the sloop *Merchant* and tried to wave to those onboard, to no avail. Crowley watched as two men were plucked from the water, but the sloop pulled away without rescuing him. That night, he tried to stay awake but eventually slept. The next day, Wednesday morning, he awoke less fatigued but hungry and parched. He floated all Wednesday, and as the sun set and he faced the prospect of a third night on his soggy raft, the cotton bale came aground in the early evening at a spot near Baiting Hollow, New York, fifty miles from where the Lexington burned and sank. Stiff and frostbitten, Crowley tumbled off the bale and, seeing a light in the distance, managed to walk three quarters of a mile to the home of Matthias and Mary Hutchinson, who took him in and cared for him.

CHAPTER 4

A TRAVELING STATESMAN

The *Lexington* disaster remains the most serious loss of life on the waters of Long Island Sound, and it was reported in newspapers around the country. It was such a historic event that in subsequent decades, many papers covered the anniversaries of the tragedy, often focusing on the remarkable escape of second mate David Crowley. Among the dead were Stonington residents Elias Brown Jr., Charles H. Phelps and Mr. Van Cott, manager of the American House hotel.[47] But in January 1840, news of the conflagration was slow to reach shore. In Stonington, the *Lexington* did not arrive when expected, but nothing else was known. Word of the fire and sinking did not get back to New York until Wednesday afternoon, January 15, when it was reported that only three people survived, because David Crowley's fate had yet to be discovered.

For days after the disaster, New York was abuzz with conflicting stories about the episode, and as a result, what was possibly the first illustrated extra was published, featuring the lithograph of the burning *Lexington* shown in the previous chapter and reporting what was known at the time about the tragedy, including a list of those who had perished. The demand for the extra was almost limitless. Newsboys sold it on the street, and copies were sent to other cities. Presses ran around the clock, and almost overnight, the small firm that produce it, N. Currier, Lith. & Pub. of Spruce Street in New York—later known as Currier and Ives—became a national institution.[48]

Drawing of Daniel Webster, circa 1897. *Library of Congress LC-DIG-pga-02400.*

DANIEL WEBSTER, THEN A United States senator from Massachusetts, had recently returned from a long trip to Europe. He arrived in New York Harbor on December 29, 1839, but by January 13, the day the *Lexington* began its last journey, he was back in Boston, where he gave a speech about agriculture in Europe.[49] Soon after, he began the long trip down to Washington, D.C., and on January 17, he was at the Steamboat Hotel in Stonington, enjoying the hospitality of Colonel Bowen Capron.[50]

Daniel Webster was a prominent Boston attorney who'd won cases in the United States Supreme Court, and in 1836, he sought the nomination of the Whig Party for president of the United States, losing to William Henry Harrison. When Harrison won the presidency on his second attempt in November 1840, he would appoint Webster secretary of state, and Webster would serve in that role again under Millard Fillmore from 1850 to 1852. But in mid-January 1840, he was just a U.S. senator trying to make his way to Washington.

One might ask: Why did a prominent politician stay at the Steamboat Hotel when more comfortable accommodations could be found at the Wadawanuck? The surviving accounts indicate that Webster had also been a visitor at the American House when "storm bound" on his way to New York.[51] Why would a man of such stature want to board on the seedier west side of the borough rather than seek more fitting rooms up the hill? There are at least two possible explanations. First, Webster was continuously in debt. He engaged in land speculation in the mid-1830s, and according to one biographer, he was plagued by substantial debts from 1837 through the end of his life.[52] Rooms at the Steamboat and American House hotels were cheaper than at the Wadawanuck.

But perhaps a more likely explanation implicates spirits. Webster was widely known as a prodigious drinker, and drinking was a popular activity on the west side of town. An account by Emma Palmer reports that "Capt. Dean delighted to tell of [Webster's visit to the American House] and said he could drink more brandy straight than any man he'd ever seen."[53] Webster would die in 1852 of cirrhosis of the liver. In Stonington, drinking was an activity more readily accomplished at the American House or in the saloon of the Steamboat Hotel.

When he arrived in Stonington, Webster's progress south was delayed by the demise of the *Lexington*. To make matters worse, there was a substantial depth of snow on the ground. As a result, Capron hired Russell Wheeler to take Webster to the Groton Ferry by horse-drawn sleigh, but they did not go directly to the river. According to Grace Denison Wheeler, "Finding themselves chilled, they stopped at the Inn at Mystic to warm both the outer and the inner man."[54] In New London, Webster would have been able to get a steamer to New York. Regular steamship transportation between Norwich, New London and New York began in 1836.[55]

ANOTHER CONNECTION BETWEEN STONINGTON and Daniel Webster appeared almost ninety years after his death. In 1936, one hundred years after Webster's failed presidential campaign and four years before the centenary of the *Lexington* tragedy, Stephen Vincent Benét, poet, playwright, short story writer and twice winner of the Pulitzer Prize, published his most famous short story, "The Devil and Daniel Webster," in the *Saturday Evening Post*. The story valorizes Webster, whom the narrator describes as having been the biggest man in the country: "He never got to be President, but he was the biggest man." The great orator and attorney comes to the aid of a struggling New Hampshire farmer, Jabez Stone, who has sold his soul to the devil in return for seven years of good crops. Webster agrees to be Stone's lawyer and demands that his client be given a trial, with a predictable result.

"The Devil and Daniel Webster" expressed a number of patriotic themes, and it won the O. Henry Prize in 1936. Benét adapted it both as a play and as a folk opera, and he worked on the 1941 film adaptation, originally released as *All That Money Can Buy*, which won an Academy Award for best original score. Many other adaptations for radio, film and television followed, including an episode of *The Simpsons* called "The Devil and Homer Simpson," in which Homer sells his soul to the devil in return for a donut.

Four years after publishing "The Devil and Daniel Webster," and one hundred years after the living hero of that story was briefly stranded in Stonington, Stephen Vincent Benét bought the famous Amos Palmer House on the corner of Main and Wall Streets in the borough. A century earlier, the house had been home to Major George Whistler's family, including the young James McNeill Whistler.

Left: Undated photo of Stephen Vincent Benét. *Underwood Archives/UIG/Bridgeman Images*

Right: Stephen Vincent Benét grave site in Stonington Cemetery. *Wikimedia.*

Benét died of a heart attack in New York City just four years after buying the Palmer House, but it remained in the family until the 1980s. Benét is buried in the Poet's Corner section of Stonington Cemetery, just a few steps from Stonington's other Pulitzer Prize–winning son, poet James Merrill.

CHAPTER 5

A STEAMBOAT FAMILY

s soon as David Crowley arrived at Matthais and Mary Hutchinson's house on Long Island, he asked his hosts to go back down to the shore and retrieve the cotton bale that had been his salvation. Mr. Hutchinson went off into the night but was unable to locate the makeshift raft. Crowley implored him to try again, and on the second attempt, Mr. Hutchinson returned with the soggy bale of cotton. Crowley kept the cotton bale for over two decades, as a bulky souvenir of his odyssey, but when cotton became a scarce commodity in the North during the Civil War, he was persuaded to sell it. According to one published account, the firm that purchased the cotton bale wove it into "Lexington Cloth" and launched a popular Lexington brand of cotton goods.[56]

In early March 1840, a month and a half after the *Lexington* burned, David Crowley was still recuperating in the home of Matthais and Mary Hutchinson in Baiting Hollow, New York. He was tended to by a doctor who initially thought his severe frostbite would require amputating his feet, but in the end, only one toe and part of another were removed.[57]

On March 4, 1840, Crowley wrote a letter to Captain John States of Stonington, and although Crowley was from Rhode Island, it is clear from the letter that he had developed an attachment to the borough: "I have not heard anything from Stonington or from the inhabitants since I left there last. I would very much like to hear from there." After he completed his rehabilitation, Crowley returned to service as a baggage mate on various boats on Long Island Sound, a career that he pursued for another fifty years. Most important to our story, according to the U.S. Census, by

An 1852 portrait of David Crowley painted by Samuel Lovett and William Jewett. On each side of Mr. Crowley are small vignettes of Crowley on his cotton bale (*left*) and of the *Lexington* on fire (*right*). Provenance unknown. *Courtesy of the Rhode Island Historical Society.*

1850, David Crowley was living in Stonington's Steamboat Hotel and had married Colonel Capron's daughter, Dorcas. Furthermore, they had a two-year-old son named David.

Initially, Capron had been running the hotel without a formal arrangement, but in 1845, Gilbert Wheeler leased the hotel to him for six years, for "use of Public House, Tavern or House of Entertainment in all of which businesses said Capron binds himself." Wheeler was only responsible for replacing windows "broken by storm or tempest." According to the lease, Capron was allowed to build a twenty-four-by-twenty-six-foot addition to the building, which, at the end of the lease, either Wheeler would buy at its appraised value or Capron would move elsewhere. The 1879 borough map shows a small ell at the rear of the building facing the railroad tracks, and the structure is also visible in an 1885 picture of the hotel (see page 28). David and Dorcas lived in this section of the building, perhaps with the senior Caprons. It is not clear what became of Mr. Capron's addition to the house, but by the time the building was lifted to its three-story height in 1888, the addition was gone.

Despite the arrival of a child, love did not run true for David and Dorcas. They were married on August 27, 1845, when Dorcas was seventeen years old and David was approximately twenty-eight, but in April 1856, David filed for divorce on the basis of infidelity.[58] According to the petition, Dorcas was caught in an indiscretion with Alexander Lyman Holley in September 1854 "and at other times." Holley was a recent graduate of Brown University, and this episode was particularly embarrassing because at the time of their affair, Holley's father, Alexander Hamilton Holley, had just finished a term as lieutenant governor of Connecticut and had ambitions of becoming governor. It is unknown how Dorcas and Alexander got together, but early in his career, the younger Holley was interested in the railroads and made a number of innovations to locomotives.[59] Of course, David's work on the steamboats meant he was away from home at predictable intervals, and Dorcas was living in a hotel filled with little private rooms. The divorce documents that survive mention Holley by name, but his name has been scratched out in several places in what appears to be an effort to cover up this episode and avoid a political scandal for the senior Holley. David's petition requested a divorce and custody of their child, David Bowen Crowley, who was approximately nine years old at the time.

A week after David filed for divorce, Dorcas filed her own petition with the court claiming that David was verbally and physically abusive, had been unfaithful to her and was "guilty of intolerable cruelty."[60] Dorcas's petition, which may have been filed in an attempt to retain custody of her son, was later withdrawn, and both parties were ordered to appear in superior court in Norwich a few weeks later. Dorcas failed to appear, and David was granted a divorce and custody of his son.

Alexander Hamilton Holley achieved his goal of being elected governor in 1857, and his son became an accomplished mechanical engineer who brought Bessemer steelmaking processes to the United States. He was so revered that, when he died in Brooklyn in 1882 at the age of forty-nine, several engineering professional organizations combined forces to sponsor the construction of a monument and bust in Holley's honor in Washington Square Park.[61]

Of course, as a practical matter, David Crowley could not raise his nine-year-old son alone. He was employed as a crew member on the New York boats of the Providence and Stonington Steamship Company, which meant he spent many nights away from home. Dorcas's father, Colonel Capron, died in 1858, but her mother, Susan, continued to operate the Steamboat Hotel for a short time after his death. In 1860, Dorcas, now thirty, and young

A bust that is part of a monument to Alexander Lyman Holley in New York's Washington Square Park. The sculptor was John Quincy Adams Ward, and the architect was Thomas Hastings. *Wikimedia.*

David Crowley, twelve, were living with her in the hotel. Furthermore, by then, David Sr. was remarried to Sarah M. Arnold, with whom he'd had a second child, Charles, who was one year old. David and Sarah were married two years after the divorce, in July 1858, in Jersey City, New Jersey, and in 1860, David's second family was living just a block away from the Steamboat Hotel on Pearl Street. David's mother-in-law, Sarah Hadwen Arnold, and an Irish servant, Catherine Fallon, were also living with them. Despite losing custody of her son in the divorce proceedings, Dorcas ended up raising young David Crowley, and it appears that, at least for a time, his father remained part of his life even after his remarriage. But the proximity of the two families did not last long.

The main terminals of the Providence and Stonington Steamship Company were Stonington, Providence, Boston and New York, and at various points in his life, David Crowley lived in all four places. By June 1865, the Civil War was over and David had moved his family from Stonington to

Left: Ambrotype portrait of Sarah M. Arnold Crowley, possibly taken in the 1860s. *Courtesy of the Nantucket Historical Association, PH169.*

Right: Tintype of Sarah Hadwen Arnold, approximately 1870. *Courtesy of the Nantucket Historical Association, PH160.*

Brooklyn. Catherine Fallon (age fifty) and Sarah Arnold (age seventy-one) were still with them, Charles was five years old and the family had welcomed a new infant, Mary. Unfortunately, Mary did not live a full year, and as an indication of David and Sarah's connection to Rhode Island, they took her to Providence to be buried.

For many years, the family lived in a brownstone on Leffert's Place, one block off Atlantic Avenue, in what is now the Clinton Hill neighborhood of Brooklyn, but David also boarded in Providence when his work required it. The 1867 Providence city directory lists him as "mate steamer Electra, house at Brooklyn." In September 1871, Sarah Arnold died. Sarah Hadwen's husband, Oliver Arnold, was from Troy, New York, and their daughter Sarah M. (Arnold) Crowley was born in New York. But Sarah and Oliver were married in Providence in 1827, and when it came time to lay Sarah Arnold to rest, Sarah and David decided on Providence's North Burial Ground, the same cemetery where they'd buried their daughter Mary. One imagines that her son-in-law, the steamship freight clerk, might have supervised the transfer of her body.

Above: An 1865 photo of the *Electra* steamboat at the Fox Point pier in Providence, Rhode Island. David Crowley was a freight clerk on the *Electra* in the late 1860s. *Courtesy of the Providence Public Library.*

Right: Advertisement from the 1875 *Boston Directory* showing information for both the Stonington Line, with steamers *Rhode Island*, *Stonington* and *Narragansett*, and the Providence line, with steamers *Galatea* and *Electra*. As evidence of its popularity, the Stonington Line got top billing and was served by more and bigger steamboats than the Providence line. David Crowley probably worked on many of these boats, but we know that he worked on the *Electra* in 1867.

1174   STEAMERS.

PROVIDENCE AND STONINGTON

Steamship Company,

BETWEEN

BOSTON AND NEW YORK.

STONINGTON LINE!

Steamboat Express Train

Leaves the Depot of the Boston and Providence R. R., (Columbus Avenue and Park Square,) daily, (except Sundays,) at 5.30 P. M., Connecting at Stonington with the new and superb
Steamers RHODE ISLAND, STONINGTON, and NARRAGANSETT, Arriving in New-York at 6 A. M.

NOT A TRIP MISSED IN SEVEN CONSECUTIVE YEARS.

Elegant Reclining Car Chairs on Steamboat Express Trains.

PROVIDENCE LINE!

Passengers leave the Depot of the Boston and Providence R. R. (Columbus Ave. and Park Square,) at 2 P. M. daily, (except Sundays,) Connecting at Providence with the staunch and powerful
Steamships GALATEA and ELECTRA.

These Steamers leave Providence at 5.30 P. M., affording passengers a full night's rest and a delightful sail through Narragansett Bay by daylight, arriving in New-York the next morning.

Rates of Fare Less than via any other Line.

Freight via either Line at Lowest Rates guaranteed, and Through Bills of Lading given.

For information, Rates, Tickets, Staterooms, &c., apply at the Company's Offices.
    J. W. RICHARDSON, Agent Stonington Line, 228 Washington St.
    GEO. C. MORRELL, Agent Providence Line, 205   "   "

GENERAL OFFICES, No. 177 WEST STREET, NEW-YORK.

L. W. FILKINS, General Passenger Agent.
               D. S. BABCOCK, President.

In 1880, nine years after Sarah Arnold's death, the Crowleys—David, Sarah and Charles, now twenty-one—were still living on Leffert's Place in Brooklyn with a different Irish servant, but at the end of that decade, the family experienced a number of changes. Beginning in the 1880s, the Fall River line emerged as the premier form of travel between New York and Boston. Under the management of the Old Colony Railroad, the line launched a new series of steamboats, each larger and more lavish than the last. In 1883, the line introduced the *Pilgrim*, a 390-foot-long iron-hulled vessel and the first American steamboat to be lit entirely by electric light, and in 1894, the 440-foot *Priscilla* was launched and soon became the most admired of the Fall River line, favored for its beautiful North Italian Renaissance interior. The *Priscilla* had a capacity of 1,500 passengers, and at the peak of the boat's popularity, it often sold out.

The Fall River line eventually crowded out the Stonington Line altogether. After a brief interruption in service during World War I, regular steamboat service to New York continued from both Providence and Fall River until 1937, when the Depression, a series of labor disputes and inexpensive rail competition shuttered steamboat companies all over the country. But because Stonington was merely a way station and not a population center and because the Fall River line was such a popular alternative for Boston-bound travelers, the Stonington line was abandoned in 1900.

It appears that Charles Crowley traveled for a few years and then, when he was thirty years old, moved to Nantucket Island in Massachusetts, where, in February 1889, he opened a real estate and insurance brokerage in a building on Main Street that had previously been a barbershop. At some point between 1889 and 1893, all three of the Crowleys left New York, and for reasons history has yet to reveal, Sarah Crowley went to live with her son on Nantucket rather than with her husband. Sarah died of pneumonia on January 15, 1898, at the age of sixty-six and was buried in Prospect Hill Cemetery on Nantucket. She and David never divorced.

WHEN CHARLES WAS VERY young, his mother had a rich uncle on Nantucket. William Hadwen was born in Newport, Rhode Island, in 1791, the third of six children; Sarah Arnold Crowley's mother, Sarah Hadwen Arnold, was the fourth. William arrived in Nantucket when it was a thriving whaling port and began a silversmith business.[62] He married Eunice Starbuck in 1822. (Starbuck was a common name on Nantucket long before Herman Melville gave it to the first mate of the *Pequot* in his 1850 novel *Moby-Dick*.)

Portraits of William Hadwen by William Willard, circa 1850, and of Eunice Starbuck Hadwen by an unknown artist, possibly Frederick Mayhew. *Courtesy of the Nantucket Historical Association, accession numbers 1905.0038.001 and 1915.0023.001, respectively.*

William later teamed up with Nathaniel Barney—the two men were cousins and business partners, and both had married Starbuck sisters—to form a whale oil and candle business, and he became known both for his business success and for his community philanthropy. In 1846, William built a Greek Revival mansion on the corner of Main and Pleasant Streets that today is a museum operated by the Nantucket Historical Society. At the time it was built, the design of the house, with its imposing Ionic columns, was considered ostentatious in relation to the simpler Quaker-style dwellings on the island. The Hadwens entertained often in the house and were generous hosts.

Charles remembered visiting Nantucket with his parents when he was very young, and it's possible he stayed at William Hadwen's house on Main Street while he was there. It's likely Sarah Arnold visited her brother on Nantucket, bringing her daughter and grandchild with her, but Charles would have been very young. William Hadwen died in 1862, when Charles was two years old, and Eunice died two years later, when he was four. The couple had no children of their own, and in 1864, the house was inherited by Joseph Barney, the only son of Hadwen's business partner and cousin. Hadwen House stayed in the family until the early twentieth century, and as a result, there may have been remaining family connections that attracted the Arnold-Crowleys to the island long after William and Eunice Hadwen

Charles Crowley, the Nantucket tax collector, with an unidentified woman at the doorway of the Old Town Building (2 Union Street) in Nantucket, Massachusetts, circa 1900s. It is possible the woman in the photo is Charles's wife, Annie Crowley, but her identity is lost to history. *Courtesy of the Nantucket Historical Association, PH168.*

died. As further evidence of a continuing link to Nantucket, a brief item in the January 4, 1879 edition of the Nantucket *Inquirer and Mirror* reads in full: "In response to an item that recently appeared in our columns, fourteen books of a miscellaneous character, have been forwarded to the 'Sconset Sunday School by Mrs. David Crowley, of Brooklyn, NY."[63]

For several years, Charles's real estate and insurance business was reasonably successful, and eventually, he was elected the island tax collector, a post he held for ten years, resigning in 1906. In his early years on the island, Charles was a baseball enthusiast, and in an era when the north and south sides of Main Street often played each other—or "crossed bats," as the local newspaper put it—he gained a reputation as one of the best pitchers on the island.

On October 17, 1899, Charles married Annie A. (Henry) Patterson of the Jamaica Plain section of Boston. The ceremony was held in the Charlestown neighborhood where Annie had been born to immigrant Scottish parents and was officiated by William R. Campbell, "minister of the Gospel."[64]

Charles was forty, and Annie was thirty-seven; this was her second marriage. Her previous marriage to Frederick L. Patterson had produced two children but ended in divorce. Charles's mother had died the previous year, which meant he no longer had any immediate family on the island. How Charles and Annie met is unknown, but in 1899, Charles, Annie and Annie's eight-year-old son Harold Patterson began a life together on the island. Two years after Charles and Annie were married, Claire Patterson, Annie's older child, a clerk in Boston, married Henry B. Thompson Jr., a "shipper." She was eighteen, and he was twenty-one.

LIKE HIS FATHER, CHARLES Crowley had difficulties in marriage, but unlike his father, his difficulties played out in the pages of a small-town newspaper hungry for material. On September 19, 1900, just eleven months after their wedding, the couple welcomed Sarah M. Crowley to their family, the third Sarah in as many generations. Now they were a family of four, and things went smoothly for a few years. But at some point, troubles emerged. According to Charles, no harsh words ever came between him and his wife until her son Harold Patterson started coming home "in an intoxicated condition" and Charles refused to have him in the house. The couple began living apart, which meant that Annie lived with the children and Charles lived alone.[65] On several occasions, Annie went to court in an effort to get Charles to pay more in support of her and Sarah.

On December 30, 1912, Annie Crowley died of pneumonia. She was fifty years old, and her death set off a confusing and dramatic legal battle. As Annie had been a longtime resident of Jamaica Plain, her funeral and burial were held in Boston, and the Reverend William R. Campbell of the Highland Congregational Church, the same man who had married Annie and Charles, conducted the funeral.[66] In a strange turn of events, the Probate Court of Nantucket appointed Harry Marshall Gardiner of the island as Sarah's temporary guardian, and she was sent to the mainland to live with relatives. Charles claimed that he had not been informed of Gardiner's petition for guardianship and that Gardiner, Mrs. William F. Codd, also of Nantucket, and the probate judge had all conspired "in the loss of his child's affections."[67] Charles obtained legal representation and brought a $30,000 suit against Gardiner, Codd and the probate judge, an amount equivalent to $895,000 in 2022 dollars. By March, the matter was resolved. Charles was appointed his daughter's guardian, and he dropped his suits against the three alleged conspirators; Sarah returned to Nantucket to live with her father.[68]

Despite this rocky beginning to Charles and Sarah's life together, the available evidence suggests that Sarah finished out her high school years happily on the island. She was particularly talented in embroidery, winning a number of competitions for her work, and she was an excellent dancer. In April 1915, she and partner Gordon Chase competed for a five-dollar prize in a glide waltz contest at the Somerset Club. According to the report in the *Inquirer and Mirror*, "Mr. Chase and Miss Crowley were quickly chosen the winners and given the gold piece by the president of the club."[69] She went to the mainland after graduation, and on September 15, 1923, four days before her twenty-third birthday, she married William Hemeon in Nashua, New Hampshire, his home town. The couple made their home in Stoneham, Massachusetts, a suburb north of Boston, and at the time of their marriage, William was a salesman and Sarah a clerk.

Sarah Hemeon's marriage was different from that of her parents in at least two important ways: she and William never separated or divorced, and they had no children. They lived modestly in Stoneham, where William worked various jobs, including gardener at a golf course and clerk at a hardware store.

IN HIS LATER YEARS, Charles Crowley appears to have had a solitary life on the island. For a time, he lived on Coatue, an undeveloped spit of land on the north shore of the island that he called Lonelyville, but eventually, he moved back to town, where he lived in a small cottage on North Liberty Street.[70] He had a catboat, which on one occasion was stolen and later recovered. In February 1918, a brief newspaper story, "Narrow Escape from Drowning," reported that while walking back home to Coatue over ice, Charles fell through when he was fifty feet from shore: "No assistance was near and Mr. Crowley had considerable difficulty in getting out and was obliged to walk two miles in wet clothes until he reached his house."[71] As his father had seventy-eight years earlier, Charles Crowley managed to avoid a watery demise in the dead of winter.

Charles occasionally wrote for the *Inquirer and Mirror* newspaper, both brief notices about the seasonal return of robins to Coatue, which reportedly happened sooner there than elsewhere on the island, and longer works of allegorical fiction that commented on the political issues of the day. Near the end of his life, he suffered from a heart ailment and rarely left his home. He died in his sleep on May 15, 1934, at the age of sixty-four and was found by neighbors the next day. Charles Crowley, the second son of David Crowley, born on Pearl Street in Stonington, Connecticut, was buried next to his mother, Sarah A. Crowley, in the Prospect Hill Cemetery on Nantucket.

HAROLD PATTERSON ENLISTED IN the army, and as of December 22, 1917, he was a private in the Sixth Infantry stationed at Chickamauga Park, Georgia. On July 10, 1918, Harold boarded a steam-powered troop transport ship leaving Hoboken, New Jersey, for Europe. He was identified as being in charge of field artillery. There is no obituary for Harold in the Nantucket papers, and I've found nothing about him beyond this point. The transport ship that took Harold Patterson to fight in World War I was named the USS *Narragansett*.

SARAH HEMEON INHERITED THE little cottage on North Liberty Street, and at least until 1978, she and William regularly visited the island in the summer, sometimes staying as long as two months. The North Liberty Street property

The U.S. Navy troop transport ship USS *Narragansett*, which took Harold Patterson to World War I, shown here aground on the Isle of Wight on February 1, 1919. In the distance is the British troopship *Empress Queen*, also aground. *U.S. Naval History and Heritage Command photograph, catalog # NH 45640.*

was on the border of what is now the Lily Pond Preserve, and in 1988, Sarah sold the property to a land trust for $190,000. She died the following year at the age of eighty-eight, and William died five years later. Sarah M. Hemeon and William Hemeon are both buried in Prospect Hill Cemetery on Nantucket. They were the last of the Crowley-Arnold-Henry/Patterson-Hemeon wing of David Crowley's family.

TWO NOTEWORTHY THINGS HAPPENED to David Crowley in 1893. First, he announced his retirement from a long career as baggage and freight clerk on the Stonington and Providence Steamboat Line. Because he was a well-known figure, particularly in Rhode Island, this event was covered on page one of the January 19 *Providence Daily Journal*.[72] Much earlier, in August 1881, the *Daily Journal* reprinted what seems to be a somewhat overblown description of him that originally appeared in the *Boston Traveler*:

> *That Mr. Crowley has become a favorite with the passengers over the Sound is not to be wondered at. His urbanity and courtesy have won him hosts of fans among the traveling public. More than this, he makes no distinction, and the poorest emigrant aboard the steamer Narragansett receives as much attention from him as the occupant of the highest-priced stateroom.*[73]

As part of the retirement announcement, the newspaper provided a brief summary of the *Lexington* disaster—now more than fifty years in the past—and Crowley's harrowing escape from death on a cotton bale. There was also passing mention of Charles B. Smith, one of the other *Lexington* survivors, who had, until recently, worked as an engineer at the Hope Street pumping station in Providence and still lived in the city.

Two months later, David Crowley happened to be a passenger on the Stonington boat train headed to Boston when the train was involved in a serious crash. In the early morning hours of March 1, before reaching Pawtuxet Village, near Warwick, Rhode Island, some of the coaches separated from the train, causing an hour-long delay. A brakeman was sent back with a flag to signal to the oncoming Shoreline Express from New York, but to no avail. The New York train crashed into the rear of the boat train, "smashing the carriages into kindling wood."[74] Several people were injured on the boat train, and a nine-month-old infant was killed.

The accident was covered extensively by the *Boston Daily Globe*, and probably because he was a well-known figure—particularly on the Stonington boat train—Crowley was recognized as "the noted survivor of the *Lexington*" and interviewed at some length:

> *I was never in a railroad accident before. I was in the middle car of the boat train. In this car was the baby that was killed. Its crying annoyed the passengers so that many went forward. I thought the child would go to sleep, so I laid down in my seat to take a nap. Next I remember was a crash. I was struck by the arm of the seat. The floor and seat seemed to fly up against me. I climbed out of the mess of baggage and broken wood. I got this bad eye by the smashup. If I'd gone ahead I wouldn't have had this eye.*[75]

The article mentioned that David Crowley was living at 12 Shawmut Street in Boston, in what is now the theater district, and that he had a pension from the New York, New Haven and Hartford Railroad—which makes sense, given that the steamship lines were owned by the railroads. David Crowley had just seven more years to live, and near the end his life, he would reconnect with his first family and his son David Bowen Crowley.

CHAPTER 6

LIQUOR IN THE BOROUGH

As we have seen, in the early era of steam, alcohol was an important offering at both the American House and the Steamboat Hotel, but these were far from the only locations where intoxicating beverages could be found. The 1881 Stonington town directory listed no fewer than eight licensed liquor dealers, and the frequent reports of police raids and of liquor arrests and seizures make it clear that illegal sales were also common.

Most of this activity happened in the northwest quadrant of the borough, in the vicinity of the steamboat landing and rail yard. Water Street, running north and south, splits the peninsula of Stonington Borough vertically. Of the eight licensed dealers in 1881, two were on Water Street, and the rest were west of Water Street. Despite Stonington being a dry town for much of the period covered by this history, liquor always found a way to survive in the borough. The saloons and hotels were in a constant battle with a very active nineteenth-century temperance movement, and nowhere was this conflict more visible than at the Steamboat Hotel.

FROM THE BEGINNING, AMERICA had a reputation for drink. According to Daniel Okrent, author of *Last Call: The Rise and Fall of Prohibition*, "The ship that brought John Winthrop to the Massachusetts Bay Colony in 1630 had more than ten thousand gallons of wine in its hold and carried three times as much beer as water."[76] During the Revolutionary war, troops were allotted four ounces of whiskey a day, and by 1830, it was estimated that the per capita consumption of pure alcohol in the United States amounted to seven gallons per year. When you factor in all the people who did not drink at all, it is not difficult to imagine the effects of all that alcohol, and it is easy to understand how calls for temperance—which initially simply meant moderation—got underway.

Neal Dow, a successful businessman from Portland, Maine, was a particularly effective campaigner for the cause of temperance. P.T. Barnum, whose American Museum in New York City featured a popular morality play called *The Drunkard; or, The Fallen, Saved*, credited Dow with turning him into a teetotaler.[77] But Dow's greatest achievement came in 1851 when, after being elected mayor of Portland, he convinced the state legislature to pass a law prohibiting the manufacture, sale or storage for sale of intoxicating liquors. The law authorized searches and seizures of illegally held liquor, and it established substantial punishments for offenders, including imprisonment after a third offense.[78] Anti-liquor laws had been brought to the Maine legislature nine previous times, but Dow's advocacy was credited with the success of the first state prohibition law in the nation.

The Maine Law, as it became known, started a wave of prohibitionism, and in the subsequent years, twelve more states passed similar laws, including New York, Massachusetts and Connecticut. Connecticut's version of the Maine Law went into effect in 1854, but in August 1872, the general assembly passed an amendment to the Act Concerning Crimes and Punishment that moved the state in the direction of regulation—licensing—rather than complete prohibition of the sale of liquor. It required that "spiritous and intoxicating liquors, ales and lagers" only be sold by licensed individuals. There was a substantial fee required to obtain a license, and licenses had to be renewed annually. The act also spelled out the requirements for maintaining a license, which included prominently displaying the license in the tavern or establishment and not knowingly selling to "drunkards" or their husbands or wives. Finally, and most importantly, licenses could only be issued in towns that had voted to allow the licensing of the sale of alcohol.[79] In the same year, Connecticut also passed a "blue law" prohibiting gambling and the sale of alcohol on the "Sabbath or the Lord's Day."[80]

As a result of the act of 1872, Stonington, like every other town in the state, was required to conduct an annual election, typically in early October, in which electors (Black and white men) would elect town officers

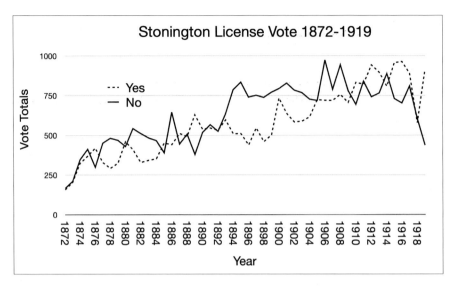

The results of license votes in Stonington town elections from 1872 to 1919. *Stonington town records.*

and vote on the question of licensing liquor sales for the coming year. As a result, Stonington fluctuated between being a technically dry town and an officially wet one, and the outcome of the license question was often the headline item in the *Stonington Mirror*'s story reporting the election results. In most of the elections between 1872 and 1920, when federal prohibition went into effect, Stonington voted "no license," but on those few occasions when the town went from dry to wet—as it did in the election of 1887— the same issue of the *Stonington Mirror* that reported the election results typically included public notices of several applications for licenses to sell alcoholic and intoxicating spirits. The 1881 town directory showing eight licensed purveyors of liquor happened to be published in a wet year.

Okrent characterizes the larger national contest over drink as being a battle of "native-born Protestants against everybody else."[81] Rural states were stronger supporters of prohibition, and newer immigrants, who were more likely to be Catholic or Jewish—religious groups for which wine had sacramental uses—generally opposed prohibition. When it came time to ratify the Eighteenth Amendment establishing a national prohibition, Connecticut and Rhode Island—both heavily Catholic—were the only two states to reject the amendment.

Locally, license votes were held at the town level. As it is today, the Borough of Stonington was only one of five districts in the larger Town of Stonington,

LICENSE BY 226

STONINGTON SHOWS PRESENT CONDITIONS NOT IN FAVOR

Stonington Has Big Republican Majority, Groton Goes Democratic.

Headline of the October 7, 1915 front-page story in the *Stonington Mirror* reporting the results of the town election. The previous year's result had been "no license." *Courtesy of the Stonington Historical Society.*

Connecticut. The borough itself was often closely divided between "license" and "no license," but the Pawcatuck neighborhood near the Rhode Island border was more heavily populated by Irish and Italian Catholics who were more favorable to licensing. Technically, the vote totals were just a recommendation to the town selectmen, who had the final say, and in 1876, the first year the town voted to license liquor sales—by a margin of 120 votes—the selectmen rejected the voters' recommendation, keeping the town dry. For the next few years, the town returned to "no license" votes.

Over the forty-eight years of votes on this issue, "no license" won thirty-three times, and "license" won only fifteen times. The results were quite close in the 1870s and 1880s, but the margins of victory for "no license" became much larger during the 1890s, after the formation of the Anti-Saloon League and other national organizations that turned the campaign against alcohol into a mass movement. Ironically, in the 1910s—the years just before prohibition became law—a resurgent "license" contingent in Stonington enjoyed a few victories.

LATE NINETEENTH-CENTURY TEMPERANCE ADVOCATES in Britain understood the importance of providing meeting places and activities as alternatives to the natural sites of social and civic life—public houses. As a result, temperance coffeehouses and temperance hotels were established to cater to teetotalers, and when billiards became a popular activity—most often played at pubs—temperance billiard halls were introduced.[82]

The temperance movement was very active in the borough and surrounding areas. Indeed, starting in 1866, the *State Temperance Journal* newspaper was published in New London, Connecticut, just fifteen miles to the west and in the same county as Stonington. The 1872 New London city directory listed a temperance restaurant on Bank Street, and in the 1880s, Stonington Borough had no fewer than four temperance organizations and its own temperance billiard hall. Lewis' Temperance Billiard Hall was at 65 Water Street, well south of the bars, and like today's Alcoholics

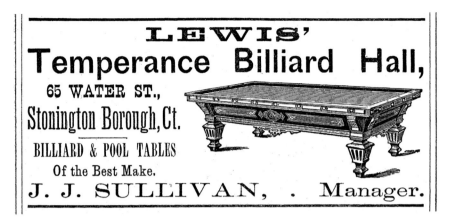

Advertisement for Lewis' Temperance Billiard Hall from the 1881 Stonington town directory, published in a "license year" when the town allowed the sale of alcohol by licensed individuals. *Courtesy of the Stonington Historical Society.*

Anonymous, the temperance societies—which met on Water Street and on the east side of town—offered a schedule of evening meetings throughout the week.

CONFLICT OVER ALCOHOL BEGAN soon after the Steamboat Hotel opened. Gilbert Wheeler was a member of the Baptist church, which, both in Stonington and elsewhere, was a major force in the temperance movement.[83] In February 1846, the Stonington Baptist Church met to pass two resolutions. The first urged church members to express their "disapprobation" of the use of intoxicating liquors "either as a beverage or as an article of trade." The second was a pledge of total abstinence from both "the use and traffic of intoxicating drinks." Perhaps as a measure of the popularity of the second proposal, the surviving documents show only nine signatures.

Two and a half years later, in July 1848, William Hyde and Gilbert Wheeler—both hotel owners and members of the Baptist church—were summoned to a meeting. According to church records, Deacon Palmer asked for a vote from the congregation: "All who were desirous that brethren Hyde and Wheeler should not rent their houses for the sale of ardent spirits and that they should free themselves from all implication in the traffic would signify by rising—*Where upon all arose.*"

In response to this rebuke, Gilbert Wheeler emerged as the more diplomatic and clever of the two men. At the time, he was in the middle of a lease of the Steamboat Hotel to Colonel Capron, and as a result, after seeing the outcome of the vote, he offered that he would "respect the feeling of his brethren and that when the lease of his house should expire he would no longer rent it for the sale of ardent spirits." The church members expressed their unanimous support for this proposal by rising up again in unison. The hour had grown late, so the case of Mr. Hyde, owner of the Eagle Hotel, was put off until the next meeting.

When the time came, rather than appear in person, Mr. Hyde submitted a letter in which he berated the church and its "low barren and shattered condition…its government, discipline of its members…which has been a great grief to me and caused me many hours of solemn reflection for months past." He also complained about his pew assignment. Embellishing his remarks with similar words of displeasure, Mr. Hyde announced that he was withdrawing his "fellowship and membership" from the church. Rather than give up the sale of alcohol, he gave up on his congregation.

Gilbert Wheeler solved the problem more skillfully. Rather than follow through with his pledge to run the hotel without liquor, he simply sold the building to Colonel Capron at the end of their lease. As a result, ardent spirits continued to flow at the Steamboat Hotel, but Mr. Wheeler was free to remain a member of the congregation. Spirits also remained available at the Eagle Hotel, where former Baptist parishioner William Hyde presided, but as we learned in chapter 2, the Eagle Hotel was destroyed by fire in 1862.

AFTER COLONEL CAPRON DIED and his wife, Susan, sold the building, the Steamboat Hotel was run by Harriet Palmer, the widow of Warren Palmer. Holding up the tradition of the house, Harriet Palmer was quite effective in defending the sale of alcoholic beverages. In December 1869, a group of temperance advocates—whose members included, somewhat ironically, Dr. William Hyde, son of William Hyde, the former Baptist parishioner and proprietor of the Eagle Hotel—took it upon themselves to visit taverns in town in an effort to convince the proprietors to stop selling liquor.[84] Most establishments refused, but encouraged by the committee, the New London County sheriff confiscated liquor from the Steamboat Hotel. This episode occurred during the period after Connecticut had adopted prohibition along the lines of the Maine Law, but enforcement of the law was notoriously lax.

Perhaps as an indication of the community's attitude toward the temperance movement, Harriet Palmer was only charged with selling adulterated beverages, and the sale of liquor continued. Although the local temperance committee had been launched with great enthusiasm, eventually, a consensus emerged that it had done more harm than good, and it was disbanded.

Harriet Palmer appears to have had an excellent reputation in town. On April 6, 1871, the *Stonington Mirror* reported that when Denous Drogan, a sailmaker who was living at the hotel, took ill, he was "tenderly cared for" by Palmer. When Drogan eventually died, Palmer arranged for his burial in the cemetery at her own expense. As the newspaper put it, "That is what we call true benevolence."[85] When she died in October 1875, the notice in the *Stonington Mirror* reported that she had died at her son's home after an illness of some months. "Her funeral was solemnized this Sunday at her former residence—the Steamboat Hotel. For her kindness of heart and many deeds of charity she will be long remembered."[86]

THE PROPER MANAGEMENT OF liquor can be a challenge, and some drinking-related problems did result. In 1871, the borough passed a relatively quiet July Fourth holiday. The citizenry was spared the usual ritual of young boys ringing church bells and making other "noisy demonstrations of patriotism" on the night of the third, and the next evening, no Roman candles were set off. The otherwise tame holiday was marred by what the *Stonington Mirror* described as an "irrepressible conflict" at the Steamboat Hotel.[87] The dispute began when a Black man claimed that a fellow patron had declined to smile at him, leading him to believe the man didn't "abide by the 15th amendment," which established equal voting rights for all adult male citizens regardless of race, color or previous condition of servitude. The Fifteenth Amendment had been ratified in March the previous year. However, the *Mirror* identified the true cause of the disturbance as "distilled molasses" (rum). The fight that ensued, which the *Mirror* described as a "speedy miscegenation of knuckles, teeth, and broken noses," eventually absorbed a "son of Erin" who was passed out in a corner on the floor. The man was "aroused from his reverie" when the two combatants fell on him. The melee was quickly ended by Constable Tillinghast and one of the night watchmen before any serious damage was done.

THROUGHOUT THE LONG HISTORY of its operation, the Steamboat Hotel was one of the most reliable drinking establishments in town, and many of its operators and patrons came into conflict with temperance advocates and the law.

CHAPTER 7

A HOTEL FAMILY

D orcas Capron's first husband arrived in Stonington on clouds of steam. David Crowley was born in Providence, Rhode Island, but because he worked for the Providence and Stonington Steamboat Company, he came through Stonington often. In contrast, Dorcas's second husband seems to have had a closer connection, and there is reason to believe he may have been a family friend.

Colonel Bowen Capron was the first keeper of the Steamboat Hotel, but this was probably not his earliest experience in the hospitality business. He and Susan were from Rhode Island, and they were the first of three generations of hotelkeepers, a line of hospitality workers that would soon find its way back to Rhode Island.

In 1860, FOUR YEARS after her divorce, Dorcas Capron Crowley was living in Stonington with her son, David, just down the street from her ex-husband, his new wife and their new baby, but ten years later, everyone had scattered. The steamboat clerk had moved his second family to Brooklyn, and Dorcas was in Newport, Rhode Island. At some point between 1860 and 1867, Dorcas married her second husband, Willard Francis Hall of West Greenwich, Rhode Island. Both Dorcas's parents were born in the rural town of Coventry, which borders on West Greenwich, and as a result, W. Frank Hall, as he was known, may have been a family friend or acquaintance.

Like Colonel Capron, Frank was in the hospitality business, and his hotel background combined with the shared connection to western Rhode Island make it easy to imagine any number of ways Dorcas and Frank might have met. As an additional twist to the story, Frank adopted young David. From this point forward, David Crowley's two families separated, and David Bowen Crowley became David Bowen Hall.

W. FRANK HALL WAS a busy hotel worker and did not stay in any one job very long. As in the cases of Gilbert Wheeler and Colonel Bowen Capron, many nineteenth-century hotels were owned by someone who leased the building to a hotel operator, and over a relatively short career, W. Frank Hall was proprietor or coproprietor of two different hotels and had an important position in another. In 1850, when Dorcas was still married to David Crowley, Frank Hall was twenty-one years old and working at an unknown hotel in the town of Groton, Connecticut, just across the Thames River from the city of New London. It is unclear what his position was, but he was still new to the business. Ten years later, he was working as the steward at the Ocean House hotel in Newport, Rhode Island.

IN 1774, NEWPORT WAS the fifth-largest city in what would soon become the United States. Before the Revolutionary War, Newport was an important shipping port and a corner of the triangle trade, a system that involved bringing slave-produced cane sugar and molasses from the Caribbean to Newport, where it was made into rum in one of the city's twenty-two rum distilleries. The rum was then taken to West Africa and traded for enslaved people who were brought to the colonies. In addition, Newport's relatively cool climate made it an attractive escape from the summer heat for visitors from the south.[88] However, these features and Newport's status as the capital of the Rhode Island Colony also made it attractive to the British, who occupied the city in 1775.

Newport went into a long slump following the revolution. The combination of the war, the Embargo Act of 1807 and the War of 1812 substantially diminished trade. Meanwhile, Newport's Rhode Island rival, Providence, emerged as a major port and manufacturing center that, by 1830, was home to 126 cotton mills.[89] But the summer resort crowd never completely deserted Newport, and the city's popularity gradually rebounded during the early decades of the nineteenth century. In 1834, Newport's *Herald of the*

Top: A stereograph card photo of the second Ocean House. *Library of Congress Control No. 2018652692.*

Below: The grand veranda of the Ocean House hotel, Newport, Rhode Island. *Courtesy of the Providence Public Library, VM013_GF4450.*

Times reported that, during a single summer fortnight, five hundred people were turned away for want of accommodations.[90]

The construction of the Ocean House hotel on Bellevue Avenue in 1844 represented a turning point in the Newport summer resort business. The four-story Greek Revival structure could house three hundred guests, but it burned to the ground a year after it was built. Nonetheless, the Ocean House had been so successful in its first season that funds were quickly raised to build an even larger hotel on the same spot. The new Ocean House, which could accommodate six hundred guests, was a striking Gothic Revival structure with a sharply gabled roof, an octagonal cupola, a wide veranda and a dramatic central hallway.[91] During the Gilded Age at the end of the nineteenth century, summer in Newport devolved into a status-conscious competition among the superrich, who built progressively larger and more lavish "summer cottages" rivaling the palaces of Europe. But during the middle decades, night boats stopped in Newport on their way to and from Fall River, Massachusetts, and the city reemerged as one of America's leading resort destinations. The Ocean House was the largest and most grand resort hotel in the city.

The Ocean House hotel and others like it in Saratoga Springs and Coney Island were symbols of the increasing democratization of leisure in America, and at its peak, the Ocean House was the center of the Newport summer social scene. The hotel management hired a band from the

Detail from the "Ocean House Polka," one of four polkas composed by Carl Bergman of the Germania Musical Society for the Newport hotels, published together in 1856 as *The Season at Newport*. *Library of Congress, M1.A12I vol. 81 Case Class.*

⟫⟩DINNER.⟨⟪

SUNDAY, AUGUST 7, 1881.

Potage.

Green Turtle,   Printanière à la Royale.

Poisson.

Potatoes à la Parisienne.

 *Boiled Salmon à la Holandaise*

Releves.

Chicken, Egg Sauce,   Corned Beef and Cabbage.
Leg of Mutton, Caper Sauce,   Baked Ham, Champagne Sauce.
Beef Tongue, Sauce Piquante.

Cold Dishes.

Lobster Salade, Homard au Naturel, Chicken Salade, Smoked Tongues,
Roast Beef, Beef à la Mode, Potato Salade, Boned Capon au Truffles,
Cincinnati Ham, Chicken, Spring Lamb, Pâté of Chicken Liver with Jelly.

Entrees.

Fried Soft Shell Crabs,   Filet of Beef, Larded aux Champignons,
Spring Ducks Braisé aux Olives,   Small Pâties of Chicken à la Reine,
Croquettes of Lobsters à la Sauce Tartare,   Macaroni à l' Italienne,
Queen Fritters au Citron,   Fritot de Volaille à la Viennoise,
Breast of Spring Lamb, Breaded aux Petits Pois.

Roast.

Spring Chicken, Stuffed,   Loin of Veal Farcies,   Ribs of Beef,
Turkey Stuffed,   Loin of Spring Lamb, Mint Sauce.

Vegetables.

New Boiled Potatoes, Stewed Tomatoes, Mashed Potatoes, String Beans,
New Beets, Green Corn, Spinach, Mashed Turnips, Squash,
Boiled Onions, Cabbage, Boiled Rice, Pickled Beets, Egg Plant.

Pastry.

Whortleberry Pie,   English Plum Pudding, Rum Sauce,   Apricot Pie,
Eclairs au Chocolate,   Vienna Cakes,   Macaroons à la Jellée,
Gâteaux Assortis,   Kisses,   Rum Jelly,
Orange Water Ice,   Confectionery.

Dessert.

English Walnuts,   Filberts,   Pecan Nuts,
Watermelons,   Almonds,   Bananas,   Raisins,
COFFEE,   Crackers and Cheese,   TEA.

An example of an Ocean House hotel dinner menu from 1881. Dinner was served midday and was the primary meal of the day. This menu was accompanied by an extensive wine list that also included brandies and ales. *New York Public Library, Catalog ID b16981665.*

Germania Musical Society and scheduled nightly concerts and dances—or "hops."[92] Newport was a major port of entry for the polka, a couples dance whose fast pace, arm-holding and popularity with the working classes scandalized the elites,[93] and the hotel offered dancing classes for new initiates.

Of course, all these hotel guests had to eat, and when W. Frank Hall was steward at the Ocean House, he would have managed the dining operation, including a large cadre of cooks, waitstaff and bussers. The hotel featured an extensive menu and an impressive wine list, and seatings were arranged on a punishing schedule. Regular guests had breakfast at 8:00 a.m., dinner—the main meal of the day—at 3:00 p.m., tea at 7:00 p.m. and supper at 9:00 p.m. Servants and children were given breakfast, dinner and tea on a separate schedule, and guests who had early boats or trains were offered breakfast and dinner two hours earlier than the usual time. For a hotel as large as the Ocean House, this would have been a great responsibility—but perhaps not as great as Frank's next assignment.

In 1863, W. FRANK Hall turned up back in Connecticut as the proprietor of the City Hotel in New London, where he remained at least until 1865. The City Hotel was a far more modest establishment than the Ocean House and, as a display advertisement in the *New London Daily Star* indicated, was designed for both "permanent or transient boarders." Abraham Lincoln is said to have visited the City Hotel before he was president,[94] but there appears to be little else that was noteworthy about the establishment—except that an important chapter of our story is likely to have happened while W. Frank Hall was there. New London and Stonington are not far apart, and Frank probably married Dorcas Capron Crowley during this period of his life.

CITY HOTEL.

State St., New London, Ct.

This Hotel is centrally located and easy of access from the Railroad Stations and Steam boat Landings, and will continue open for the accommodation of permanent or transient boarders.

W. FRANK HALL.

feb 2-tfd   **Proprietor.**

Display advertisement for the City Hotel; W. Frank Hall, proprietor; New London, Connecticut, from the *New London Daily Star*, July 22, 1865.

A photo taken on State Street in New London, Connecticut, looking east toward the train station and the Thames River ca. 1870. The City Hotel, once operated by W. Frank Hall, can be seen to the right. *Courtesy of the New London Public Library.*

By 1867, Frank had moved on, and like so many of the hotels in this story, the City Hotel was destroyed by fire in 1891.[95] The Cronin Building on State Street in New London is now were the City Hotel once stood.

From New London, Frank moved back to Rhode Island, and there, our story takes an important turn. In 1867, W. Frank Hall was the co-proprietor, with J.M. Kilburn, of the Aldrich House hotel on Washington Street in downtown Providence, and his adopted son, David Hall, was working there as a clerk. Frank was thirty-eight years old, and David was nineteen. This is the first time I have discovered David using his adoptive father's name and the first indication that David had joined the Capron-Hall family business. He would go on to surpass the previous two generations in his chosen profession.

The Aldrich House was smaller than the Ocean House but larger than the City Hotel, and it appears to have been well regarded. A group of elite fighting men, a New York regiment of Zouave soldiers known for their flamboyant French-inspired uniforms, visited Providence in 1868 when W. Frank Hall was co-proprietor of the hotel. The Zouaves arrived on the steamer *Bristol* and were greeted by Rhode Island governor Ambrose Burnside, with whom the Zouaves had fought during the North Carolina

An undated photo of Aldrich House hotel on Washington Street, Providence, Rhode Island. If you look carefully, you will see there are a remarkable number of people posing in this picture. Could one of the men standing in front of the hotel be W. Frank Hall? Or the young David Hall? *Courtesy of the Providence Public Library.*

campaign of 1861–62, acting as Colonel Burnside's bodyguards. After their arrival in Providence, the Zouaves and the governor made their way to the Aldrich House for breakfast.[96]

By 1870, Frank and Dorcas were back at the Ocean House, where Frank was once again serving as steward. The Halls remained in Newport for the next several years, but on June 13, 1875, Willard Francis Hall succumbed to tuberculosis at the age of forty-five. Hall died in Providence, where David was still working as a clerk and living at the Aldrich House, which suggests that David moved his father to Providence to take care of him at the end of his life. David would assume a similar caretaking role on several occasions.

Frank was temporarily entombed in Providence's North Burial Ground before being buried in Stonington Cemetery, not far from Dorcas's parents, Colonel Bowen and Susan Capron. His death record, for which his wife was probably the informant, listed his occupation as "hotel keeper." W. Frank Hall lived a relatively short life and was a husband and parent for less than fifteen years, but he was an important mentor to his adopted child, turning a steamboat clerk's son into a hotelkeeper.

WHEN HIS PARENTS RETURNED to Newport and the Ocean House, David Hall stayed behind at the Aldrich House, clerking at the hotel and later at a sewing machine showroom on Westminster Street. In 1877, David married Susan "Susie" Horton, and the following year, he reentered the family business as a clerk at the newly built Narragansett Hotel. The Narragansett was a seven-story red-brick building that dominated the corner of Dorrance and Weybosset Streets in the center of Providence. When it opened in 1878, the Narragansett immediately became the premier establishment in Providence[97] and remained so until the Biltmore Hotel opened in 1922. In 2012, Dr. Richard Greenwood of the Rhode Island Historical Preservation and Heritage Commission called the Narragansett "possibly the finest hotel in the city's history."[98] A traveler's guide, *King's Pocketbook of Providence*, published four years after the hotel opened, put it this way:

> *It is not the province of this work to furnish the history of hotels which have had their day: all that can be done is to enumerate the more prominent hotels of the present time and then describe the most magnificent hotel—the Narragansett—which has made Providence famous among the cities of the world having unusually noteworthy hotels.[99]*

The 225-room Narragansett Hotel had a spacious, high-ceiled lobby, a grand ballroom and an elegant dining room. At the street level on both Dorrance and Weybosset, retail shops looked out onto wide sidewalks. The lobby, mezzanine and other public areas were decorated with large old master paintings. A few of the more risqué canvases caused controversy, including one in the bar that could be seen by riders on passing trolleys.[100]

An early undated photograph of the Narragansett Hotel at Dorrance and Weybosset Streets in Providence. Later in its history, the building's smooth lines were marred by the addition of a network of fire escapes. *Courtesy of the Providence Public Library.*

The dining room was forty-five by ninety feet with a twenty-six-foot ceiling, and there was a separate lunchroom that was open to the public. Civic organizations often had dinners or luncheons at the Narragansett, and in January 1913, an exhibition of high-end Stutz motor cars was held in the ballroom.[101] Among the many famous people who stayed there were

MAIN LOBBY SHOWING STAIRCASE, NARRAGANSETT HOTEL, PROVIDENCE, R.I. (UNDER OWNER MANAGEMENT)

Postcard image of the lobby of the Narragansett hotel. *Author's collection.*

"Buffalo Bill" Cody, said to be the most well-known American of his time,[102] whose Wild West Show came to Providence in 1884, and the Providence Grays baseball team, which beat the New York Metropolitans three games to none in the first World Series that same year.[103] In December 1882, the *Newport Mercury* reported that former Rhode Island governor Charles C. Van Zandt, a native of Newport, and his wife were "domiciled" at the Narraganset for the winter.[104]

In 1880, David and Susan Hall had a daughter, Mabel Kendall Hall, and for the next twenty years, they all lived together in the hotel. By 1900, David had managed to rent the building and become the proprietor of the Narragansett Hotel. His grandfather ran Stonington's Steamboat Hotel, and his father had been the proprietor of the City Hotel in New London and the Aldrich House in Providence, as well as serving two stints as steward of the Ocean House in Newport. But David's ascension to proprietor of the Narragansett was the greatest achievement of three generations of hotelkeepers.

AFTER W. FRANK HALL's death—perhaps using family connections once again—Dorcas took up residence in the Updike House hotel in East Greenwich, Rhode Island. East Greenwich bordered on her husband's

An undated photo of the Updike House hotel on Main Street in East Greenwich, Rhode Island. Dorcas Capron Hall spent her last years here. The building is now an apartment complex with a bar and music venue on the first floor. *Courtesy of the Providence Public Library.*

hometown of West Greenwich and was adjacent to her own hometown of Coventry.[105] Alice Updike, the aging owner, also lived at the Updike, and Nathaniel Carpenter was the proprietor.[106] During this time, Dorcas occasionally returned to Stonington to visit friends.

At the end of his mother's life, David Hall brought Dorcas to Providence, where she died at the Narragansett Hotel of atherosclerosis on October 5, 1908, at the age of seventy-nine. Her death record lists her "usual home" as East Greenwich. Somewhat sadly, despite her longer and more recent marriage to Frank Hall, the brief notice of her death that appeared in the *Stonington Mirror* made no mention of him and concentrated on her famous first husband's harrowing escape from the conflagration of the *Lexington*.[107] David Hall arranged for his mother's burial next to her husband's grave in the Stonington Cemetery.

WHEN DAVID CROWLEY BANGED up his eye in the Stonington boat train accident, he was on his way home to Shawmut Street in Boston, but a few years later, he was back in Providence living on Chestnut Street downtown, within walking distance of both his old workplace on the Fox Point pier and the Narragansett Hotel, where David Hall was a clerk. In 1898, about the time of his wife's death from pneumonia on Nantucket, David Crowley was admitted to Butler Hospital, a psychiatric facility on the east side of Providence, diagnosed with senile dementia. Two years later, he died of cardiac failure at the age of eighty-three. His wife had predeceased him, and his son Charles Crowley and wife, Annie, had recently welcomed their new daughter, Sarah.

The informant for David Crowley's death record was his first son, David Hall, now the proprietor of the Narragansett Hotel. This is another moment for speculation. We cannot be certain why Sarah Crowley followed her son Charles to Nantucket rather than staying with her husband. Sarah had family on the island, and her steamboat clerk husband was often away from home. They never divorced, but are these reasons enough to explain why they lived apart in the final years of their lives? After decades of separation from his first family, David Crowley returned to Providence, the city of his birth, and when he needed care, the responsibility was assumed not by the son who still bore his name but by his first child, who had long before been adopted by another man.

David Hall buried his biological father in Providence's North Burial Grounds, next to his mother-in-law, Sarah Hadwen Arnold. When I visited David Crowley's grave, 120 years after his death, I found a small stone for a child between the monuments for David and Sarah. After so many years, I was unable to make out the inscription, but I assume the stone was for Mary, David and Sarah Crowley's child who died in infancy. Sadly, the gravestones of David Crowley and his mother-in-law were broken in half. The most famous survivor of the *Lexington* disaster, a celebrity in his day, had been all but forgotten, and his grave site was in disrepair.

SOON AFTER DAVID HALL took over the Narragansett Hotel, the family moved out of the hotel to a house on Everett Avenue on the east side of Providence, and approximately ten years later, two important events happened. Mabel married an actor, Clarence Gordon Prouty, and David Hall, now in his early sixties, retired from the hotel business.

Clarence Prouty, who adopted the stage name Jed Prouty, was born to wealthy Bostonians and claimed to have run away to join the circus. He made his stage debut at the age of fifteen at the Boston Museum theater,

Above: Undated photograph of the Providence Opera House on Dorrance Street in Providence, the premier theatrical venue in the city. The seven-story Narragansett Hotel can be seen to the right of the opera house. *Courtesy of the Providence Public Library.*

Opposite: Jed Prouty and Spring Byington in a publicity still from the 1940 Jones Family film *Young as You Feel. 20ᵗʰ Century Studios. Author's collection.*

and when he heard the audience's applause that night, he decided to make acting his life's work.[108] As with so many couples in this story, it is impossible to know how Mabel Hall and Clarence "Jed" Prouty first met, but there were three active theaters near the Narragansett Hotel, and the Providence Opera House, the city's premier theatrical venue, was next door. By the time Mabel and Jed crossed paths, Prouty was beginning a successful acting career, and it is quite possible he met Mabel at the Narragansett Hotel while performing in Providence.

What we know for certain is that Mabel Hall married Clarence "Jed" Prouty in Manhattan, New York, on June 7, 1911.[109] Mabel was thirty-one years old, and Jed was thirty-two. David Hall maintained his house on Everett Avenue in Providence through the 1910s, but in 1919, David and Susan moved to Manhattan to live with their daughter and son-in-law on West Eighty-Second Street on the Upper West Side. The 1920 census

identified David Hall, age seventy-one, as the head of a household that included Susan, Mabel and Jed. It is impossible to know for certain, but the truth may be that the younger couple took in Mabel's aging parents. In any case, Mabel appears to have lived with her parents for much of her life.

When Mabel and Jed met, Prouty was beginning to have his first big successes in what would be a very long career. After learning the ropes in vaudeville, he became a very effective character actor in musical comedies. In June 1910, a year before marrying Mabel Hall, Prouty made his Broadway debut in a production of *Girlies* by Frederic Thompson at the New Amsterdam Theatre. The *New York Times* said, "Jed Prouty, who doesn't look or act like his name sounds, reveals a pleasing voice in a pretty little Irish song."[110] In November 1914, he appeared in a production of the musical *Only Girl* starring Wilda Bennet and Thurston Hall at the Thirty-Ninth Street Theatre, and in September 1916, he appeared in the musical comedy *Miss Springtime*, which the *New York Times* described as "a triumph."[111] *Miss Springtime* ran for 224 performances.[112] In 1917, Prouty was cast in a patriotic film, shown at the Strand Theatre, promoting sales of the World War I Liberty loan, and the *New York Times* reported that in addition to Prouty, Douglas Fairbanks, Will Rogers, Lillian Russell and Ethel Barrymore appeared in the film.[113] In 1919, Prouty began his transition to film, with roles in two silent movies that year.

In August 1919, the Actor's Equity Association declared a strike against the increasingly monopolistic producers who had imposed a number of controls on actors' jobs and compensation, including unlimited unpaid rehearsals. A photo of Prouty participating in an automobile parade in support of the strike appeared in the *New York Evening World* newspaper on August 12. The strike ended on September 6, with the actors winning almost all their demands.

In less than two years, between 1919 and 1920, the Hall-Prouty family faced a series of tragedies. In the strike parade photo in the *Evening World*, Prouty is standing next to a tonneau-style open-seat automobile, and later that month, he, his wife, Mabel, and his mother-in-law, Susan, were in his own tonneau automobile on their way to a dinner party when three boys ran out from behind a van on Eighty-Third Street between Broadway and West End and were struck by Prouty's car, which was being driven by a chauffeur. Ten-year-old James Smith was killed immediately. According to one news report, Mabel screamed, and she and Susan left the car "in a bad state of nervous excitement."[114] They were taken away from the scene by women from the neighborhood. Meanwhile, Jed put another boy, the six-year-old George Black, in his car and took him to Roosevelt Hospital. Both the other boys survived with minor injuries, and after Prouty and other witnesses testified to the chauffeur's innocence, the police did not charge him.

The next two tragedies dealt the family far more serious blows. On January 24, 1920, Susan Hall died in Roosevelt Hospital subsequent to an operation. She was seventy years old. The brief report in the *Providence Daily Journal*, "Wife of David B. Hall Dead at New York City Hospital," described her as a "well-known resident here for many years."[115] Then, one year and eleven months later, Mabel Prouty died of endocarditis, an inflammation of the inner layer of the heart.[116] She was forty-one years old.

In less than two years, both David Hall and Jed Prouty were widowed, and David lost his only child. David buried his wife and daughter in the beautifully maintained Swan Point Cemetery in Providence, overlooking the Seekonk River, where many prominent Rhode Islanders have been interred. He marked their graves with a single rose-colored marble headstone, leaving room for his own name to be added later.

Jed Prouty moved to Los Angeles to continue his film career, and when the talkies came, he made a smooth transition. Rarely a leading man, Prouty became a popular character actor, recognizable by his trademark round spectacles, and made 149 appearances in films and television series over a career that extended into the early 1950s.[117] Prouty achieved his greatest fame for the role of patriarch John Jones in the Jones Family series of family comedies, B films designed to be the second feature in a double bill. The series ran for seventeen installments, with Jones appearing in all but the last.

On August 23, 1923, Jed Prouty married his second wife, actress Frances Marion Murray, in Los Angeles, and in 1930, they were living together on Hollywood Boulevard. Jed's profession was listed in the census as actor in "talking pictures," and Frances was unemployed.[118] However, in 1936–37, using the stage name Marion Murray, Frances played both Cleopatra and the Spirit of '76 in a successful Broadway musical revue, *The Show Is On*.[119] She had small roles in two films in the 1940s: the 1941 World War II

A still from the 1943 patriotic feature *A Stranger in Town*, starring Frank Morgan, who played the Wizard in *The Wizard of Oz*; Jean Rogers, best known for her portrayal of Dale Arden in the *Flash Gordon* serials; and Richard Carlson. *Left to right*: Rogers, Marion Murray, and Carlson. *Metro-Goldwyn-Mayer. Author's collection.*

espionage thriller *Paris Calling*, starring Elisabeth Bergner, Basil Rathbone and Randolph Scott, and the 1948 Judy Garland and Gene Kelly musical, *The Pirate*.[120]

Marion Murray (Prouty) died in New York on November 11, 1951, at the age of sixty-six, and Clarence "Jed" Prouty died on May 10, 1956, at the age of seventy-seven. Prouty's was the lead obituary in the *New York Times* the following day, running to half a column and featuring a photo from the 1939 film *Quick Millions*. The obituary made no mention of his first wife, Mabel Prouty.

AFTER THE DEATH OF his wife and daughter, David Hall returned to Providence to live once again in the Narragansett Hotel. In 1923, he came out of retirement to take a position in a new hotel in Portland, Maine, but a year later, he returned to Providence to assume a position as one of the assistant managers of the newly constructed Biltmore Hotel.

Providence's Biltmore hotel (now the Graduate Providence). When it opened in 1922, it replaced the Narragansett Hotel as Providence's premier establishment. *Wikimedia.*

Photo of the Aldrich House hotel taken the day after it was destroyed by fire. *Courtesy of the Providence Public Library.*

David Hall was born in a hotel and died in a hotel. A life that began at Stonington's Steamboat Hotel ended at Providence's Biltmore Hotel when David Hall succumbed to Bright's disease on January 18, 1926, at the age of seventy-five, ending a chain of three generations of hotelkeepers that included his grandfather, Colonel Bowen Capron, and his adoptive father, W. Frances Hall. The following day, his obituary ran on page two of the *Providence Daily Journal* and included the only portrait of him known to survive. The *Journal* described him as the "dean of hotel men" and summed up his life this way:

> *During his long connection with the Narragansett Hotel, he met practically all the notables who visited the city. Presidents and prima donnas, soldiers, and the outstanding figures in political, professional, and business life were all counted among his friends.*[121]

DAVID B. HALL, DEAN OF HOTEL MEN, DEAD

Member of Managerial Staff of Biltmore Hotel Was in His 75th Year.

WAS BORN AT STONINGTON

Portrait and headline from David Hall's obituary in the *Providence Daily Journal,* January 19, 1926.

On the night of February 15, 1888, the temperature in Providence dropped to twelve below zero and a fire broke out on the Washington Street block where the Aldrich House hotel stood. Guests and staff where shuttled to nearby City Hall to escape the flames and cold, and an Aldrich House bartender started handing out drinks until the fire chief stopped him. The fire hoses left ice everywhere, and the *Providence Daily Journal* reported that the firemen had to chop each other out of their beards.[122] The building was a total loss and was never rebuilt.

Ten years later, on September 9, 1898, the Ocean House hotel in Newport was destroyed for the second time in a spectacular blaze. It had been the last of the resort-era hotels in the city and was by then something of an anachronism, a vestige of a different kind of summer by the sea.[123] The Ocean House was never rebuilt. Today, on Bellevue Avenue, an interpretive sign placed by the Newport Historical Society identifies the spot where the hotel once stood. It is now occupied by a strip mall.

The Narragansett Hotel continued on for several more decades. It even managed to keep serving alcohol during prohibition, but the lower level was heavily damaged by flooding during the hurricane of 1938. The lobby fell into disrepair in the 1950s, and the hotel closed in 1959. In 1960, the building was demolished to make way for a parking garage.[124]

CHAPTER 8

A RESTAURANT FAMILY

The November 5, 1870 edition of the *Stonington Mirror* included an advertisement for a "LADIES' AND GENTLEMEN'S RESTAURANT, Where may be found all the Delicacies of the season."[125] The restaurant was at "No. 19 Gold Street," which was the Steamboat Hotel's address at the time, and the proprietor of the restaurant was identified as "M. M. Barnswell." Although this is the period when Harriet Palmer owned the building, Margaret Barnswell had a restaurant at the Steamboat Hotel and may also have been the hotelkeeper. The same advertisement offers "furnished rooms connected with the establishment."

Margaret M. Barnswell was an African American woman whose skills in the restaurant business were honed in Brooklyn, New York. In December 1852, her husband, Thomas R. Barnswell, with a partner, took over the City Hall Lunch at 337–339 Fulton Street in Brooklyn. A December 28, 1852 advertisement in the *Brooklyn Daily Eagle* announcing the change of management promised "GAMES, POULTRY, AND OYSTERS served at the Saloon at all times." This must have been a successful enterprise because thirty years later, Thomas and Margaret's son, Thomas F. Barnswell, was described by the same newspaper as "a colored man of means, whose father formerly kept a large restaurant on Fulton street."

Thomas R. Barnswell was born in 1807 in Edenton, North Carolina, in a state that did not abolish slavery before the Civil War, and as a result— were it not lost to us—the story of Thomas's youth and migration north would be of great interest. In 1840, at the age of thirty-four, he was living

LADIES' AND GENTLEMEN'S

RESTAURANT,

Where may be found all the Delicacies of the season, and you will be served in the best possible manner

FURNISHED ROOMS

connected with the establishment.

M. M. BARNSWELL, Prop'r.

No. 19 Gold street, Stonington.

CITY HALL LUNCH,

337 and 339 Fulton street, Brooklyn,

Kept by the late John Boorman, has been taken by
T. BARNSWELL & D. ROSELL.
The Establishment has been refitted in the neatest manner; the Larder will be furnished with the best the market affords—GAMES, POULTRY, and OYSTERS, served at the Saloon at all times; and parties supplied with BONED TURKEY, Chicken, Sallad, and Pickled Oysters. Walters provided. The favor of the public is solicited.   d2 1m*

Top: Advertisement for Margaret Barnswell's restaurant in the Steamboat Hotel in the *Stonington Mirror*, November 5, 1870. *Courtesy of the Stonington Historical Society.*

Bottom: Advertisement announcing Thomas R. Barnswell's assumption of the management of Brooklyn's City Hall Lunch restaurant (with a partner) in the *Brooklyn Daily Eagle*, December 28, 1852.

in Manhattan's eleventh ward with a person who was identified in the U.S. Census only as a "free colored female"—presumably Margaret, age twenty-three. The couple had five children: Ruth, born in approximately 1839, Thomas Francis in 1841, Paul Gustavus in 1844, Matilda in 1846 and Ashea Lavinia in 1848. The trails of Ruth and Matilda go cold very quickly, and it may be that they did not live long. This theory is further supported by an 1884 foreclosure action on property owned by the estate of Thomas R. Barnswell that listed only Margaret and three children—Thomas F., Paul and Ashea—as his descendants.[126] Thomas R. Barnswell died on March 22, 1864, and as far as we know, Margaret never remarried.

OUR STORY TOOK AN important turn when Ashea Lavinia Barnswell married a boy from Stonington, Connecticut. In 1860, William Henry Wood—known as W. Henry Wood—was a nineteen-year-old steamboat waiter living with his mother and several siblings in the borough, and according to the New York State Census, in 1865, Margaret and her children Thomas, Paul and Ashea were all living together in Brooklyn. However, by 1870, six years after Margaret Barnswell's husband died, she was living with her married daughter and son-in-law in Stonington and operating a restaurant in the Steamboat Hotel. Furthermore, Ashea and Henry had welcomed a new child, Thomas—the third Thomas in three generations of Barnswell-Woods.

Once again, it is impossible to know how a young man from Connecticut met a Brooklyn girl, but steamboats must have been involved. The food service connection could also have played a role. Census records do not reveal exactly where the family was living, but it was near the hotel. Although Black people were employed at the Steamboat Hotel, my research has not revealed any Blacks ever living there. This is somewhat different than the pattern seen at larger hotels, where Black staff members often lived in the building. At the time Margaret opened her restaurant, Harriet Palmer was living in the hotel, but Margaret and the rest of the Barnswell-Wood family were living in a different house nearby. However, thanks to the *Stonington Mirror*'s report of the July Fourth "irrepressible conflict" described in chapter 6, we know that Black people were served at the Steamboat Hotel.

Henry Wood appears to have been an enterprising person and, perhaps in part because he grew up in Stonington, a well-liked member of the community. Often, when he and Ashea welcomed a new child into their family, the news was reported in the *Stonington Mirror*.[127] Years later, when Silas Wood, one

HOME RESTAURANT !
Opposite the Steamboat Landing,
STONINGTON, CONN.
Meals at all hours. Board by the day or
week, with or without rooms.

———

Also, connected with the establishment
Pleasant Ice Cream Parlors,
With Private Rooms for Parties.
Every attention shown to guests, regular or
transient.
W. HENRY WOOD, Manager.
June 18, 1874.

Advertisement for a restaurant operated by W. Henry Wood in the *Stonington Mirror*, August 27, 1874. *Courtesy of the Stonington Historical Society.*

of Henry's sons, returned to town to become an assistant to John W. Wagner, a local barber—or "tonsorialist," as the *Mirror* called him—this was also reported in a small news item. Although he was by then a young man, Silas was identified as a "borough boy."[128]

As is typical of many of the Black people in our story, Henry Wood changed jobs relatively frequently. Keeping up the family tradition, in 1874, he ran a restaurant in town called Home Restaurant.[129] The location of this establishment is unclear. A newspaper advertisement describes it as "opposite the steamboat landing," which could indicate the Steamboat Hotel, but the local city directories of the period identify Mrs. Barnswell as the proprietor of a saloon and restaurant at the Steamboat Hotel until at least 1876.

BY FAR THE MOST interesting member of the Barnswell-Wood family appears to have been Thomas Francis Barnswell, Margaret Barnswell's eldest son. One of his most noteworthy accomplishments happened relatively early in his life. In 1862, this Brooklyn-born son of the woman who would later run a restaurant at the Steamboat Hotel became the first African American to graduate from Wesleyan University.[130] Although higher education had been available to white men for two hundred years, the first African American to graduate from a college in the United States was Alexander Lucius Twilight, who got his degree from Middlebury College in 1823. In 1850, Oberlin College became the first to award a bachelor's degree to an African American woman, Lucy Ann Stanton.[131]

Colleges in Connecticut were slow to open their doors to the education of African Americans, and after an earlier student was harassed by white students and left Wesleyan, the trustees passed a resolution in 1833 stating that "none but male white persons shall be admitted as students to this institution."[132] The resolution was rescinded two years later, but it was not until 1860 that Wilbur Fisk Burns, the son of a Liberian Methodist bishop, became the first Black student to graduate from Wesleyan, followed by Thomas F. Barnswell, the first African American, in 1862. Amos Beman, son of the minister of the African Methodist Episcopal Zion church in Middletown, Connecticut, who had himself been harassed on campus when he was tutored by an abolitionist Wesleyan student, visited Barnswell a month before commencement and described Thomas as "another…star of our race."[133]

In 1870, just as Margaret Barnswell was opening her restaurant in Stonington, Thomas was also living in the borough, but not in the Barnswell-Wood household. He was living with the Stephen Carter family. Carter was a sixty-year-old "private cook," and his son James, age thirty, was also living at home and working as a cook. Thomas was twenty-nine years old, and his occupation was listed as "student," which is consistent with a Wesleyan alumni record indicating that in the 1870s, Thomas both worked as a bookkeeper in Stonington and studied law in nearby Mystic, Connecticut.[134] In eighteenth- and nineteenth-century America, legal education was often based on an apprenticeship system,[135] and it appears that, while working as a bookkeeper in Stonington, Thomas studied law with an unknown attorney in Mystic. It is also quite likely Thomas worked for his mother in some capacity, because in 1871 he took the unusual action of suing his own mother.

The *Stonington Mirror* account of the case merely refers to Thomas F. Barnswell as the plaintiff and Margaret Barnswell as the defendant, but in a small town like Stonington, everyone would have recognized this as a son suing his mother. Thomas was asking for ninety-six dollars in wages, and Margaret presented a "set-off," which probably amounted to some other form of compensation. Both parties were represented by counsel, and Justice Greenman found for the defendant, awarding Margaret fifty dollars plus court costs.[136]

Not long after this court case, on July 2, 1872, Thomas married Alice Elizabeth Reed of Bath, Maine.[137] How this couple met and where their wedding took place is lost to history. According to Wesleyan University alumni records, Alice gave birth to Thomas Albert Barnswell in February 1874; however, the boy died six months later.

In addition to providing Thomas with a career, his education in law seems to have led to a long history of personal involvement in the courts. This unfortunate case in Stonington was just the beginning of a line of suits he brought against various individuals, and on more than one occasion, he was obliged to come before the bar as a defendant. But despite the census identifying him as a "student," Thomas may have been doing some teaching during his time in Stonington, because an 1877 notice in the *Mirror* indicated that "Prof. Barnswell is engaged in collecting soldiers' bounty and pension claims"[138] and encouraged any soldiers entitled to a pension to "see Thomas." It is also possible the title "Prof." was simply an honorific—or sarcastic—reference to his level of education. Soon after this, which also appears to be around the time his mother closed her restaurant in the Steamboat Hotel, Thomas returned to Brooklyn.

BECAUSE THOMAS WOULD QUITE frequently find his way into the pages of the newspaper, we know more about him than we do about his younger brother, but based on a variety of sources, we also have the outlines of the life of his brother, Paul.

The American Missionary Association (AMA) was a Protestant abolitionist group founded by Lewis Tappan in 1846, whose goals were not merely the end of slavery but also to bring the full benefits of citizenship to African Americans. Although education was not its only mission, the AMA established more than five hundred schools and colleges, including Fiske, Hampton, Atlanta and Howard.[139] After the Emancipation Proclamation went into effect in 1863, the AMA intensified its efforts to build schools and send teachers to the south to educate the freedmen. The teachers recruited for this effort included some educated northern Blacks, and one of these was Paul Gustavus Barnswell.

Paul's educational history is unknown to us, but his brief time with the AMA warranted mention in Clara Merritt DeBoer's *His Truth Is Marching On: African Americans Who Taught the Freemen for the American Missionary Association, 1861–1877*. In 1865, Jonathan Jasper Wright, a teacher and law student who would go on to become the first Black associate justice of the South Carolina Supreme Court, set up a school for the Black soldiers of the 128th Regiment at Camp Station, approximately a half mile from Beaufort, South Carolina.

DeBoer takes the story from here:

> *Wright's assistant, until he proved too weak to withstand the temptations of camp life and succumbed to drink, was African American Paul Gustavus Barnswell of Brooklyn, New York. Barnswell had offered to produce testimonials from most of the prominent black men in the nation and several white ones, when he applied for a commission. He protested his innocence when he resigned, saying that a bar "detached from the house" where he lived with his brother in town, was the probable reason that AMA Superintendent Richardson thought his brother's house was not a fit place*

to stay. Barnswell was an example of a black man who had had the advantages of a northern education but who proved a failure in the work at the South. Such failures could also be catalogued for the white teachers as well, of course.[140]

DeBoer's account treats Paul rather harshly. From this distance, it is impossible to determine whether he was guilty of anything at all, but what we know about the rest of his life provides no hint that he had "succumbed to drink" or that he was a failure. In contrast, his Wesleyan-educated older brother did run into trouble with the law on more than one occasion, but neither of the Barnswell brothers was the kind of failure that DeBoer suggests Paul represented.

The brother mentioned in DeBoer's account is most likely Paul's older brother, future Stonington resident Thomas F. Barnswell. Although there are some gaps in Thomas's trail during this period, we know that he returned to Brooklyn after graduation from Wesleyan, because in July 1863 he registered for the Civil War draft. He gave his occupation as "saloon," which suggests he was working for his father. In August 1863, he made a claim of $600 in damages to property at 50 New Chambers Street in lower Manhattan resulting from the previous month's draft riots.[141] Thomas's name appeared in the *New York Times* in a separate list labeled "Additional Claims Made by Colored People." Thomas may also have spent some time working with the AMA in the south, but by June 1866, both brothers were in Savannah, Georgia, working at the Freedman's Hospital under the supervision of surgeon Alexander T. Augusta.[142]

ALEXANDER THOMAS AUGUSTA WAS an important figure in the history of medicine and the Civil Rights Movement in the United States. Augusta was born a free man on March 8, 1825, in Norfolk, Virginia. From an early age, he wanted to become a doctor, but because it was illegal to educate Blacks in Virginia, he learned to read secretly and, in the 1840s, moved to Baltimore to continue his studies by hiring private tutors while working as a barber.[143] He applied to the University of Pennsylvania to study medicine but was denied admission and moved to California to make money during the gold rush. Having faced nothing but roadblocks to his education in the United States, Augusta eventually moved to the more tolerant environment of Toronto, Ontario, and enrolled in Trinity Medical College at the University of Toronto, receiving his bachelor's degree in medicine with full honors in 1856.

An undated photograph of Dr. Alexander Augusta (1825–1890). *Universal History Archive/UIG/Bridgeman Images.*

Augusta stayed on in Toronto to serve as the administrator of the university hospital, but he returned to the United States in 1862. In January 1863, soon after Lincoln's Emancipation Proclamation went into effect, Augusta wrote President Lincoln, requesting an appointment as surgeon (all physicians were commonly called surgeons) for one of the Black regiments of the Union Army, and in April, he was granted a commission at the rank of major. This accomplishment made Augusta the highest-ranking Black man in the Union army and the first Black doctor in the army. Nonetheless, Augusta continued to experience prejudice, and his commission caused confusion among many white soldiers, who found it difficult to accept a Black man of higher rank. At his first assignment, with the Seventh U.S. Colored Infantry at Camp Stanton, Maryland, the other white surgeons, who were of lower rank, were so upset by his presence that they wrote to the White House and the War Department complaining about this "humiliating" situation and succeeded in getting Augusta transferred to a hospital for African American soldiers at Camp Barker in Washington, D.C.[144]

While in the District of Columbia, Augusta was involved in a somewhat famous civil rights episode. On February 1, 1864, Augusta was on his way to the hospital to pick up some notes prior to testifying as a witness in a court martial proceeding, and as he attempted to board a streetcar at Fourteenth and I Streets, the conductor informed him that he could not enter and must ride on the front of the car "as it was against the rules for colored persons to ride inside."[145] Refusing this indignity, Augusta tried to enter the car anyway, and the conductor grabbed him and threw him off the platform. He was forced to walk in mud and rain and arrived late to court.

Augusta described this incident in great detail in a letter of complaint to the assistant secretary of war, pointing out that Black streetcar passengers were asked to pay the same fee as white passengers but were not allowed access to the cars. The letter came at a fortuitous moment, because U.S. senator Charles Sumner, a staunch abolitionist from Massachusetts, had just proposed a bill to prohibit discrimination against Blacks on the district's railcars. Sumner received a copy of Augusta's letter and, in a fiery speech, read it on the Senate floor, adding that "an officer of the United States with the commission of major, with the uniform of the United States, has been pushed off one of these cars on Pennsylvania Avenue by the conductor for no other offense than that he was black." The legislation passed, ending this kind of discrimination on streetcars in Washington, D.C.[146]

Despite this local success, thirty years later, in what is considered one of the worst decisions of the United States Supreme Court, seven justices held that it was constitutional for the State of Louisiana to deny Homer Plessy a seat in a "whites only" railroad car because he was an "octoroon," one-eighth black, which meant that in Louisiana he was considered "colored." *Plessy v. Ferguson* institutionalized discrimination in many public settings by codifying the fiction of "separate but equal."[147]

After the war, Augusta was hired by the medical division of the Bureau of Refugees, Freedmen and Abandoned Lands (commonly known as the Freedman's Bureau), which provided food, clothing, legal aid and medical services to freed slaves and poor whites of the south. He was put in charge of Lincoln Hospital, the newly established freedmen's hospital in Savannah, Georgia, where, according to records kept by the Freedman's Bureau, in June 1866, both Thomas and Paul Barnswell were employed.

Whatever trouble he might have gotten into in South Carolina, by February 25, 1866, Paul had been hired by Dr. Augusta at a salary of thirty dollars a month in a position listed as "clerk."[148] By at least June, Thomas was also working at Lincoln Hospital, at the same pay rate. In comparison to other employees, this was a very good salary. For example, out of the thirty-nine other hospital employees listed on the June 1866 ledger page where "T. F. Barnswell" also appears, only one other person, the "hospital steward," equaled Thomas's salary. Among the other employees on the page, including nurses, cooks, bakers, laundresses and guards, salaries ranged between six and fifteen dollars a month. A "ward master" was listed at twenty dollars a month.[149]

The fairness of pay rates was a particular concern for Dr. Augusta. During the Civil War, white privates were paid $13 a month, and Blacks were paid $7. When he was commissioned in 1863, Augusta was assigned a salary of $169 a month, the rate for a surgeon at the rank of major, but in early 1864, the army paymaster refused to pay him more than $7. Always the activist, Augusta wrote to Senator Henry Wilson of Massachusetts, chair of the Military Affairs Committee, protesting the inequality of pay for Black and white soldiers. Although the new policy did not go into effect

	LIST OF MEDICAL OFFICERS.				
NAME.	RANK.	STATION.	PRESENT OR ABSENT.	BY WHAT AUTHORITY PLACED ON DUTY.	
A.T. Augusta	Surgeon	Savannah	Present	Bvt Maj Genl Sexton	
C.H. Taylor	Ast Surgeon	"	"	"	
G.W. Southwick	" "	"	"	Brig Genl Tilim	
P.G. Barnswell	" "	"	"	"	
J.M. Phinizy	" "	"	"	"	

A page from a weekly report of the Freedman's Bureau for March 10, 1866, showing the medical officers for Lincoln Hospital, Savannah, Georgia. A.T. Augusta is listed as surgeon, and three names down, P.G. Barnswell is listed as an assistant surgeon. *National Archives (Washington, D.C.).*

until June that year, Congress finally established equal pay for soldiers, regardless of race.

It's clear that Thomas and Paul Barnswell were considered valued employees. Of course, by 1866, Thomas had been a college graduate for four years, which must have set him apart from almost all the other employees at the hospital. DeBoer's account of Paul's work with the American Missionary Association suggests that he also had some level of education. In addition, a weekly report of the Freedman's Bureau for March 10, 1866, includes a list of "Medical Officers" of the hospital.[150] The top medical officer was "A. F. Augusta, Surgeon," and among the four remaining medical officers, all listed as "Asst. Surgeon," is "P.G. Barnswell." It is unclear what duties fell to assistant surgeons at Lincoln Hospital, but less than a month after he was hired, Paul was holding a position of some stature.

In 1868, Alexander Augusta returned to Washington, D.C., and a year later, he was hired as one of the founding faculty of the medical college of Howard University, giving him another distinction: the first Black medical professor in the United States.[151] Dr. Augusta died in 1890 at the age of sixty-five, and after a life with many "firsts," in death, he became the first Black officer-rank soldier to be buried in Arlington Cemetery. His friend and colleague Dr. Anderson Abbott said of Dr. Augusta that he "stirred the faintest heart to faith in the new destiny of the race."[152]

By 1870, WHEN HIS mother and older brother were in Stonington, Paul was back in Brooklyn and had started a family. He was twenty-six years old and married to the twenty-two-year-old Emma Fredenburg, and the couple had produced two children, Paul (three) and Cecilia (one). Paul and Emma would go on to have a total of five children, several of whom eventually married and started their own families.

In 1870, Paul Sr. reported his occupation as "restaurant keeper," suggesting that, for a time at least, he returned to the family business. But from 1874 on, Paul was identified in the census and city directories as a musician and music teacher, beginning in Brooklyn but soon moving to Manhattan. Once in Manhattan, the Barnswell family made a slow migration uptown. In various sources, they are first on West Twenty-Sixth Street, in what today is the Chelsea neighborhood, and then moving on to West Twenty-Ninth and, later, East Eighty-Eighth.

Paul Gustavus Barnswell died of tuberculosis in Manhattan on November 23, 1892, at the age of forty-eight. His occupation was given as "musician," and he was buried in the Evergreens Cemetery in Brooklyn. Emma Barnswell never remarried and soon continued the migration northward through Manhattan, making her last residence on West 118th Street in the center of Harlem. Well into the new century, Emma remained active in the Lincoln Literary and Musical Association, which author Craig Steven Wilder described as an "elite social club" for Black New Yorkers.[153] She frequently served as an officer of the association, helping to organize its

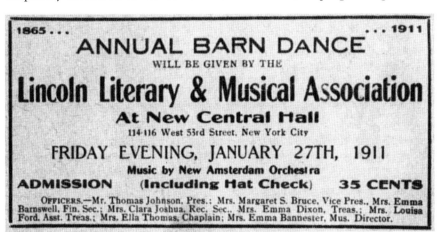

An advertisement for the annual barn dance of the Lincoln Literary and Musical Association showing Mrs. Emma Barnswell as financial secretary. This ad appeared in a newspaper for African Americans, the *New York Age*, on January 26, 1911.

annual dances and banquets. After an illness of six months' duration, Emma died on January 19, 1927, at the age of seventy-six. The occupation listed on her death certificate was "housework."

ALTHOUGH PAUL BARNSWELL WENT directly back to Brooklyn after his time at Lincoln Hospital, we know that Thomas first moved to Stonington, Connecticut, where his mother and sister were living and that during this period he married Alice Reed. But by 1880, Thomas and Alice were living on Bergen Street in Brooklyn with Annie Reed, Alice's sister.[154] Thomas was thirty-nine, Alice twenty-seven, and Annie eleven.

After returning to Brooklyn, Thomas worked variously as a bookkeeper, realtor, attorney and physician and became a well-known figure in town. During a convention held in October 1881, he was elected secretary of the newly formed Brooklyn Colored Citizens Organization,[155] and he was also active in a Republican Colored Voters group.[156]

During this period of his life, Thomas accrued an impressive number of legal conflicts, many of which were reported in the *Brooklyn Daily Eagle*. In September 1885, he found his way into an establishment known as Sawyer's Place in Coney Island's "Gut."[157] The Gut was a notorious section of Coney Island known for drink, dancing and prostitution. According to an account in the *Eagle* entitled "ROBBED AT CONEY ISLAND: Mr. Barnswell's Unique Adventures After Night in the 'Gut,'" on the night Thomas walked into Sawyer's Place, "the piano was going, as were the dancers." Mr. Sawyer and another man invited Thomas into a back room where they said the "ladies were enjoying themselves." Thomas agreed, but the next thing he knew, he was in a darkened room where "his pockets were unceremoniously emptied." He claimed to have had $186 on him at the time, and arrest warrants were issued for the two alleged thieves. Sawyer and his accomplice were held on $500 bail and granted a continuance. The resolution of the case was not reported in the paper.

Perhaps Thomas's most unusual court appearance—even more unusual than suing his own mother—and one that may have had a pivotal effect on his marriage occurred the following January. A woman named Lizzie O'Keefe, who had been jailed for twenty-nine days on a charge of intoxication, appeared in court with her "mulatto" baby, subsequent to a petition filed by Thomas Barnswell.[158] Thomas claimed that he was the father of the child and that he should be granted custody on the grounds that the mother had "neglected to provide for it and was a dissolute woman."

Despite what may have been a well-intentioned impulse on Thomas's part, Judge Cullen decided against him and issued a harsh statement: "The man who claims to be the father of the child has no right to it whatever and cannot have it. A man who does not marry a woman has no claim on her children, though he may be the putative father." Of course, given his expressed opinion of Lizzie, it is likely Thomas had no interest in marrying her, and there was the additional complication that, as far as we know, he was already married to Alice.

Sometime during this period in the mid-1880s, there was another interesting turn in Thomas's personal life: he divorced Alice and married his much younger sister-in-law, Annie Reed. We know Thomas and Annie were married by April 1888 because—in yet another court case—the couple brought charges against their landlord at 94½ Lafayette Avenue subsequent to a physical alteration over a rent dispute.[159] Thomas alleged that during a heated argument about a missed rent payment, the landlord, David W. Harvey, broke into the Barnswell apartment, "knocked Mrs. Barnswell down and struck [Thomas] on the head with a pistol." The Barnswells sought $5,000 in damages for the assault, but the jury acquitted Mr. Harvey.

As further evidence of Thomas's new family arrangement, the 1992 New York State Census listed him, now age fifty, with the occupation of "clerk," living with Annie (twenty-two) and three young children: Nina (four), Thomas F. (three), and Paul G. (one). The last evidence I was able to find of Alice Barnswell was an 1888 city directory that showed "Barnswell, Alice E." living alone at 463 Sixth Avenue in Manhattan. The name just below hers in the directory was "Barnswell, Paul, musician," living on East Eighty-Eighth Street.

Thomas Francis Barnswell made a number of mistakes in his life, but for anyone who cares to look, the hand of racism can be seen in many of the stories reported about him in the press—nowhere more so than in the brief notice of his death published in the *Brooklyn Daily Eagle* on November 22, 1892.[160] The paper painted a story of a broken alcoholic who died "friendless and penniless," but we know that just months before he died, he was living with his wife and three children. There are several inaccuracies in the short and poorly researched obituary, which appears to have been written with the aim of creating a sense of schadenfreude in the newspaper's predominantly white readership. The article does mention that Thomas was "a graduate of a medical school and for a long period a lawyer in good practice," but contrary to the *Eagle*'s report, this was not "before his father's death." Thomas R. Barnswell, the restaurant owner, died in 1864, just two

ALL KNEW "TOM" BARNSWELL.

Death of a Character Well Known in Brooklyn for Many Years.

Tom Barnswell for many years one of the most widely known characters about the city died yesterday, friendless and penniless, at his home on Butler street, between Bond and Hoyt. His father, who was the proprietor of a hotel in the days when houses on Fulton street were few and far between, left him $75,000. This was a large sum at that time and Tom lived in real splendor until he had squandered it all. He was a graduate of a medical school and for a long period a lawyer in good practice, but this was before his father's death. With the last of his fortune he went to Florida. On his return, penniless, he found his practice and his friends gone. He drowned his sorrows in the cup which had wrought his ruin. His favorite haunt was at Adams and Willoughby streets, where he could have been found for the past many years.

The obituary of Thomas Francis Barnswell in the *Brooklyn Daily Eagle*, November 22, 1892.

years after his son became the first African American to graduate from Wesleyan University.

Thomas Francis Barnswell was fifty-one years old when he died of "pneumonia, grip," and if the dates we have are correct, he died just two days before his younger brother, Paul. According to his death report, Thomas was also buried in Evergreens Cemetery in Brooklyn, although I have been unable to find any evidence of grave markers for either Thomas or Paul.

EVENTUALLY, WE LOSE TRACK of Margaret Barnswell. Harriet Palmer, the owner of the Steamboat Hotel, died on October 7, 1875, at the age of fifty-two, but Mrs. Barnswell continued to run a restaurant in the building for at least another year and a half. In June 1877, advertisements began to appear in the *Stonington Mirror* offering the restaurant space for rent, signaling the end of Margaret's run at the Steamboat Hotel. Also in 1877, Harriet Palmer's son, Warren Oliver Palmer III, sold the hotel to Ellen Foley, about whom we will hear more later.

Although she was no longer at the Steamboat Hotel, 1877 did not mark the end of Margaret Barnswell's work in food service. The 1880 census shows Margaret, age sixty, living on Trumbull Street in Stonington with her grandson, Paul, age thirteen, the son of Paul and Emma Barnswell. It is unclear why the younger Paul Barnswell was living with his grandmother

TO LET!

The Restaurant building at present occupied by Mrs. Margaret M. Barnswell. For particulars inquire of the undersigned, residing near the premises.

DAVID S. HART.

Stonington, June 2, 1877

Advertisement in the *Stonington Mirror* on July 26, 1877. David S. Hart owned the property directly east of the Steamboat Hotel. *Courtesy of the Stonington Historical Society.*

in 1880, but one possibility is that he was apprenticing with—and helping out—his grandmother in the family restaurant business. At that time, his parents were living on Bergen Street in Brooklyn, and his father was working as a music teacher. The 1881 Stonington directory shows "M. M. Barnswell" living at 8 Trumbull Street, with occupation listed as "restaurant," but it is unclear whether the restaurant in question was in her home or elsewhere in the borough.

We know that Margaret Barnswell lived to be at least sixty-four years old, because the October 4, 1884 edition of a New York publication called the *Record and Guide* reported that she sold a piece of property on Bergen Street in Brooklyn, possibly the house that Paul and Emma occupied before they moved to Manhattan, which might also have been occupied in 1880 by Thomas F. Barnswell, Alice and Annie. Margaret and her three surviving children were listed as sellers, with both Margaret and Ashea, "Wife of William H. Wood," living in Stonington, Thomas living in Brooklyn and Paul living in "New York."[161] I've been unable to find any mention of Margaret beyond this date. It is likely she ended her days in Stonington, and she may be buried in the Wood family plot in Stonington Cemetery. But we just don't know.

IN HIS LATER YEARS in Stonington, William Henry Wood served as a constable and bailiff. In 1891, he was elected Stonington constable for the sixth consecutive time, and William Haynes described him in the *Stonington Chronology 1649–1949* as "the only Negro to hold either office in New London County."[162] At that point, Henry was the oldest member of the Stonington police force, and he received the highest vote count in the 1891 election. The Woods's oldest daughter, Mary, married John Harden, a waiter from Poughkeepsie, New York, and, as her mother had done before her, Ashea and Henry eventually moved to Poughkeepsie to live with their married daughter. William Henry Wood died on June 14, 1894, in Poughkeepsie, New York, at the age of fifty-two. In his last will and testament, he wrote,

"First, I give, demise, and bequeath to my beloved wife Ashea L. Wood my one-half share of the house situated at Stonington, Conn., known as 22 Wall Street." He bequeathed his watch and chain to his eldest son, Thomas, his "wearing apparel" to his son Silas—except his dressing gown and few other items his wife wanted—and his bookcase and writing desk to his youngest daughter, Mary Matilda Wood.

Ashea Barnswell Wood, the woman who brought her mother to Stonington and the Steamboat Hotel, died of a stroke on October 23, 1903, at the age of fifty-four. For reasons that are unclear, she ended her days at Dr. Aldrich Hospital in Fall River, Massachusetts. The occupation listed on her death record was "stewardess," which in 1903 likely meant that she carried on the family's five-decade-long tradition of restaurant work, perhaps on the steamers of the Fall River line. Although they died in Massachusetts and New York, respectively, Ashea and Henry Wood were buried in the Wood family plot in the Stonington Cemetery.

CHAPTER 9

CIGARS AND LIQUOR

A fter her death, Harriet Palmer's son, Warren, sold the Steamboat Hotel to Ellen Foley, wife of John Foley, for $2,500 on February 21, 1877. Ellen bought the hotel for her newly married daughter and son-in-law, and the Foley family owned the hotel for over four decades.

FROM THE MID-NINETEENTH TO the mid-twentieth century, Westerly, Rhode Island's greatest resource and most valuable export was granite stone, frequently used in grave markers and monuments,[163] and John Foley was an important figure in this industry.[164] Born in Galway, Ireland, in 1824, Foley came to Boston as a boy, where he apprenticed as a stonecutter. He eventually moved to Westerly to work at the Smith Granite Company, retiring after thirty-five years of service, a prominent and respected member of the local community. While living in Boston, he married Ellen Murray, and the couple produced three children: William Foley, who followed his father in the granite business, Mary Ann Foley and John Jr.

After studying at St. Joseph Convent in Hartford, Connecticut, Mary Foley married Michael F. Martin on May 13, 1875, at St. Michael's Church in Pawcatuck, Connecticut, not far from Stonington Borough. Michael was born in Ireland and had immigrated with his parents to Hartford. After the Foleys' purchase of the Steamboat Hotel, Michael became the hotelkeeper and ran several businesses in the building.

TO RENT.

In the Steamboat Hotel, a few nice rooms, furnished or unfurnished, on reasonable terms.

M. F MARTIN.

Advertisement from the October 17, 1878 edition of the *Stonington Mirror. Courtesy of the Stonington Historical Society.*

The Martin era was one of both growth and turmoil at the hotel. The Martins, particularly Mary, were ambitious and hardworking, but as the young couple entered the hotel business, a second wave of the temperance movement was gaining strength in the post–Civil War era.[165] Civic objection to the sale and consumption of alcohol in the borough reached its greatest fervor during the Martins' time at the Steamboat Hotel, bringing them into regular contact with the authorities.

In the early years of their marriage and management of the Steamboat Hotel, the Martins expanded both their businesses and their family. Mary Agnes Martin was born in 1877, John Foley Martin in 1879, Thomas F. Martin in 1882, William J. Martin in 1883 and Andrew J. Martin in 1888. In addition to running the hotel, Michael Martin operated a cigar-manufacturing business in the building. The 1880 U.S. Census shows the Martins living in the hotel, and in addition to the usual boilermakers, railroad workers and servants, three cigar makers were boarding there, one of whom was eighteen-year-old John Foley Jr., Mary's brother and Michael's brother-in-law.

The cigar business was a thriving enterprise during the Martins' early years in the borough. Advertisements for M.F. Martin's "Cigar Manufactury" appeared regularly in the local papers and directories in the late 1870s and early 1880s. In addition, Michael clearly wanted to sell liquor and appears to have done so at various points, both legally and illegally. An advertisement that appeared in the *Stonington Mirror* in 1879, a "no license" year, announced M.F. Martin's sale of "hop beer," which the Superior Court of New London (Connecticut) had held was nonintoxicating. The advertisement ends with the somewhat overblown disclaimer, "Parties in want of intoxicating liquors will please go somewhere else, as I cannot accommodate them."[166] Despite this assurance, two years later, during the license year of 1881, *Anderson's Stonington Directory* listed Michael F. Martin as one of eight licensed liquor dealers in the borough, and a display advertisement in the directory described Martin as a dealer in foreign and domestic liquors.

HOP BEER!

The above brand of beer, which has of late gained such notoriety, I have for sale and invite the public to examine, more particularly those persons who are prejudiced against the sale of liquor. This beer is warranted to be non-intoxicating, as the action of the Superior court lately held in New London will show, and parties in want of intoxicating liquors will please go somewhere else, as I cannot accommodate them.

a17-w2   M. F MARTIN.

MICHAEL F. MARTIN,

PROPRIETOR OF

Steamboat Hotel.

MANUFACTURER OF CIGARS,

AND DEALER IN

Foreign and Domestic Liquors.

19 GOLD STREET,

(Between Pearl St., and Railroad Avenue),

STONINGTON,   CONN.

Left: Hop beer advertisement in the April 17, 1879 edition of the *Stonington Mirror. Courtesy of the Stonington Historical Society.*

Right: Advertisement in the *Anderson's Stonington Directory* from 1881, a rare "license" year when the sale of liquor was legal, advertising the sale of both cigars and liquors by M.F. Martin at the Steamboat Hotel. *Courtesy of the Stonington Historical Society.*

Although Martin was involved in legal sales of spirits during a brief wet period in 1881, he appears not to have given up the business in the subsequent dry years. A January 1883 report in the *Stonington Mirror* notes that "prosecuting agent Sage has sent to the state chemist for analysis three bottles of liquor purchased by detectives at M. F. Martin's place. The bottles contained respectively whisky, rum, and cider brandy."[167]

This was a period when the Law and Order League was operating in the borough and elsewhere in Connecticut. The Law and Order League began in Chicago in 1877 as a direct response to what many citizens felt was the lax enforcement of existing liquor laws.[168] The movement soon spread throughout the country, finally becoming incorporated in 1885. The league's first founding principle was, "We believe it an admitted fact that drunkenness inflicts upon the people of this country more misery, pauperism and crime than all other causes combined."[169] But the organization stood for enforcement, not prohibition. In the view of many, corruption and political threats had encouraged law enforcement officers to look the other way when liquor laws were violated, and the Law and Order League was established to support and encourage the police. Later, the league expanded its concerns to prostitution, gambling and dealers in obscene literature,[170] and in Connecticut, the movement led directly to the establishment of a state police department in 1903.

THE YEAR 1883 WAS one of particular conflict for the Martin family. Perhaps subsequent to the discovery of spirits on his property, the Law and Order League took the unusual step of banishing Michael from the borough; however, on March 17, the *Stonington Mirror* reported that the league had voted to allow Michael Martin back in town as long as he provided a $500 bond and signed an agreement not to sell intoxicating liquors or to allow intoxicating liquors to be sold in his establishment.[171] Just a week later, when Michael was perhaps still stinging from his treatment by the league, the *Mirror* reported that "Mr. Michael F. Martin contemplates removing his family and business from Stonington to Westerly this spring."[172] But the authorities did not let up. In October 1883, prosecuting agent Sage again issued warrants to search the Steamboat Hotel and another residence on the west side of town. In this case, the investigators "were unable to discover anything contraband."[173] They had better success on November 15 when John Foley Jr. was arrested on charges of selling liquor at the Steamboat Hotel without a license and "keeping with the intent to sell." He was freed on $800 bond, but the *Mirror* did not report the resolution of his case.

Michael Martin's conflicts with authorities were not exclusively about liquor. In May 1888, the street commissioner, Charles B. Moore, notified Michael that the hotel's stoop extended too far into the sidewalk on the south side of Pearl Street, creating an obstruction, and when Michael failed to remedy the situation, Mr. Moore attempted to get the job done himself. However, when he and his assistants arrived at the building, they were greeted by Martin and allies armed with flowerpots and bats. Moore retreated without achieving his objective.[174]

THE YEAR 1888 WAS one of growth and change for the Martin family. That year, the Martins raised the Steamboat Hotel to its current height of three stories, making additional room for retail businesses on the first floor. But their greatest accomplishment of the year was the construction of a new and much larger hotel on Canal Street in Westerly, Rhode Island, very near the train station. The Martin House Hotel, as it was known, was a three-and-a-half-story brick structure with a slate mansard roof. When the Martin House opened, the Martins moved to Westerly, leaving the management of the Steamboat Hotel to John Foley Jr and P.J. Quilty, about whom little is known. The Foley and Quilty tenure was quite short, however, because on April 22, 1891, John Foley Jr. died of "a fit" (presumably a heart attack) while playing cards.[175] Quilty soon leased the hotel to Cornelius Vaughan,

A 1909 postcard image of the Martin Hotel in Westerly, Rhode Island. *Author's collection.*

who went on to apply for a license to sell liquors in October 1892.[176] That year, the pro-license voters won by a mere eight votes.

The Martin family's conflicts with the law continued when, just two weeks before her brother's death, Mary Martin was tried and found guilty of three counts of illegal liquor sales at the Martin House Pharmacy. Although Benjamin Rush, the famous Philadelphia physician and signer of the Declaration of Independence, was an early advocate for temperance and many other physicians took up the cause, some doctors claimed that wine, brandy and whiskey had legitimate medicinal uses and prescribed their use for a range of maladies.[177] In addition, the post–Civil War period saw the growing popularity of patent medicines—the majority of which were not actually patented—some of which contained substantial amounts of alcohol. When Lydia Estes Pinkham's husband suffered real estate losses in the Panic of 1873, the Lynn, Massachusetts housewife cooked up some herbs and roots in her kitchen and marketed the resulting brew as "Lydia E. Pinkham's Vegetable Compound," which she recommended for "female complaints." Pinkham was an avowed supporter of temperance, as well as an abolitionist and feminist, but the enormous success of her compound stemmed from its 20.6 percent alcohol content.[178] Pharmacies also carried an array of tonics and bitters, many of which were consumed—either consciously or unconsciously—for the buzz they provided. Later, during

Prohibition, pharmacies became a major work-around for the distribution of alcohol. Pint bottles of Old Grand-Dad whiskey were marketed with the claim "Unexcelled for Medicinal Purposes."[179]

The prohibition-era pharmacy's role in the distribution of alcohol was sometimes a source of humor. In comedian W.C. Fields's first feature film, *It's the Old Army Game* (1926), and his short film *The Pharmacist* (1933), he repeated a gag designed to evade the police. In both films, Fields played a pharmacist who sold illegal alcohol. When approached by a male customer he did not recognize, the pharmacist placed a small electric fan on the counter to blow open the lapels of the customer's coat. When the fan revealed a policeman's badge pinned to the man's vest, Fields's pharmacist struck a dignified pose and feigned insult at the suggestion that he would break the law.

Advertisement for Lydia E. Pinkham's "Vegetable Compound" to be used for all female complaints, showing a young girl wearing a red hat. *Wellcome Collection.*

Given this environment, it is easy to imagine how a pharmacy attached to a popular hotel might come under scrutiny from the law. Mary Martin was sentenced to ten days in jail, a $25 fine on each count and court costs, but she appealed the case. According to the *Stonington Mirror*, just one or two weeks prior, she had been arrested for "keeping a nuisance" and paid $1,000 bond prior to appearing in court on that charge. The article reporting these events concluded, "Apparently Westerly is a hard town in which to run a first-class hotel successfully, unless you are in the ring."[180]

The move to Westerly signaled a number of changes for the Martins. Mary emerged as the most successful businessperson in the family just as her marriage was ending. In June 1892, the Superior Court of Washington County, Rhode Island, granted Mary Martin a divorce from Michael F. Martin on the grounds of "habitual intemperance."[181] A year later, while living in Rutland, Vermont, Michael was arrested for intoxication but was allowed to go home. However, when he landed in court a few days later on the same charge, he was fined a dollar and sentenced to thirty days in jail.[182] He never remarried.

After her divorce, Mary left the Martin House in other hands and moved to Boston, where she established a corset and millinery shop on Boylston

Street, with the millinery operation under the management of her daughter Mary Agnes Martin.[183] Mary Agnes would go on to be a hat designer with one of the leading millinery houses in New York. In 1899, Mary Martin married Joseph Graf, and the couple eventually returned to Westerly to resume management of the Martin House Hotel with the assistance of Mary's youngest son, Andrew Martin.

Michael F. Martin returned to Stonington Borough, where he died of pneumonia on March 4, 1900, after a brief illness. He was fifty-two years old, and his last employment had been at the Atwood-Morrison machine factory in the borough.

Mary Graf died at the Martin House Hotel in the town of her birth, on February 23, 1939, at the age of eighty-two. The *Westerly Sun* newspaper ran her obituary on the front page and described her as "one of Westerly's oldest and best known residents."[184]

The Martin House still stands on Canal Street in Westerly and has been beautifully restored. The upper floors were recently converted into condominiums, and the ground floor houses retail shops.

CHAPTER 10

AN AUSTRIAN TAILOR

In September 1892, a large advertisement appeared in the *Stonington Mirror* announcing a new business in town: "SOMETHING NEW! JACOB SEIDNER, VIENNA MERCHANT TAILOR, STONINGTON, CONN." The address of Seidner's shop was given as 113 Water Street, but he later moved his business and his family into the Steamboat Hotel. A new arrival in town, Seidner would go on to become a successful merchant and a beloved member of the community.

JACOB SEIDNER WAS BORN in Vienna, Austria, in 1858. Sailing out of Bremen, Germany, Jacob immigrated to New York City in July 1888, when he was thirty years old, and worked there as a tailor. In 1889, he married Emma Beck of Philadelphia, who was also an émigré from Vienna, and—for reasons that are unknown—he brought his family to Stonington in 1892. Jacob and Emma had three children: daughters Olga and Sophie were born in New York in 1890 and 1892, respectively, and their son, Otto, was born in Stonington in 1894.

Mr. Seidner's first shop was in the main business district of the borough at 113 Water Street, but the June 11, 1897 edition of the *Stonington Mirror* reported that "a large door and display window have been placed in the north side of the Steamboat Hotel where Jacob Seidner will have a store."[185] His family also lived in the Steamboat Hotel at that time, but because the end of the nineteenth century was marked by a remarkable number of fires

SOMETHING NEW !

JACOB SEIDNER,

VIENNA MERCHANT TAILOR,

STONINGTON, CONN.

The undersigned would call the attention of his friends and the public in general, that he is prepared to execute all work entrusted to him with promptness and dispatch. First-class work guaranteed, at the Lowest Prices. Dyeing, Scouring and Cleaning by a new chemical process

JACOB SEIDNER,

VIENNA MERCHANT TAILOR,

113 WATER STREET.

CUSTOM WORK A SPECIALTY.   ALTERING AND REPAIRING.

Renovating and repairing of Seal Jackets in the Latest Styles.

Left: Advertisement in the *Stonington Mirror* from September 19, 1892, introducing Jacob Seidner's business. Five years later, he would move his shop to the Steamboat Hotel, where he and his family also lived. *Courtesy of the Stonington Historical Society.*

Below: A late nineteenth-century photo of Jacob and Emma Seidner, possibly reprinted from a cabinet card. *Courtesy of Westerly Public Library and Wilcox Park.*

in and around the hotel, his time at that location was probably more exciting than he would have liked.

On March 10, 1898, a fire broke out in the Potter Block across Pearl Street from Seidner's shop, and Jacob bravely ran into the burning building in an effort to save the baker who worked in the grocery store there. Thankfully, the baker was not in the building at the time, and Jacob escaped without injury. Nonetheless, his courageous effort did not go unappreciated, and the *Mirror* reported that Jacob's friends presented him with a handsome leather medal with silver trimmings, inscribed:

> *Presented to*
> *Jacob Seidner*
> *For Bravery at the*
> *Potter Block Fire,*
> *March 10, 1898.*

Jacob's friends purchased a policy insuring the medal for the duration of his life, and he mounted the medal on the wall of his parlor.[186]

Fire was discovered on the southeast corner of the roof of the Steamboat Hotel on May 24, 1899, at about 7:15 p.m., possibly caused by sparks from one of the passing engines.[187] An alarm was sounded by the bell on the engine house, and both the switching engine and another engine alerted the fire department by continuous blasts of their whistles. The hook and ladder company was quickly on the scene. Using their ladders, the firemen mounted the roof of an adjoining building and directed their hoses at the fire, quickly extinguishing it.

By far the most consequential fire for Jacob Seidner happened at the Steamboat Hotel in October of the same year. An oil lamp fell, starting a blaze that gutted his shop and badly burned him.[188] According to legend, this experience would affect Jacob's future choice of housing.

IN OCTOBER 1898, JACOB Seidner became a naturalized citizen of the United States. At that time, the process of naturalization simply required that you'd lived in the country for five years and that someone could vouch for your character and adherence to the Constitution of the United States. In Jacob's case, John Lee and Aaron Goldstein, both of New London, Connecticut, signed his naturalization application. There were too many John Lees in New London for us to know who this person was, but Aaron Goldstein was a haberdasher with a shop on Bank Street in New London and a member of Ahavath Chesed, New London's first Orthodox Jewish congregation. Achim Shalom, the first Jewish congregation in New London, was formed in 1878, and Ahavath Chesed was founded in 1892, the same year the Seidner family came to the area.[189]

It is an interesting question how Jacob and Aaron became acquainted. They were both Jewish, but it is unlikely that Jacob was a member of any congregation. A trip to New London, fifteen miles west of the borough, would have been inconvenient, and congregation Sharah Zedek in Westerly, Rhode Island, which was only six miles away, was not formed until 1908.[190] Because Aaron emigrated from Belarus and Jacob was Austrian, their only common language would have been English. As a result, it seems most likely they were business associates in related fields. Furthermore, we know that Jacob sold hats and caps in his Steamboat Hotel shop, so it's possible that Aaron was his supplier.

In 1898, the printed naturalization application form only anticipated male applicants—"He has behaved as a man of good moral character…"—but under the Naturalization Act of 1855, Emma Seidner—who would not gain the right to vote until 1920—became a United States citizen by virtue of her marriage to a naturalized man.[191]

It is a measure of Jacob Seidner's business success that, in 1900, a year and a half after gaining citizenship, he took his entire family to Europe for a three-month-long vacation. It is likely that Jacob and Emma wanted to visit relatives and show the children where their parents were born and grew up.

Even more remarkable than the Seidners' trip was Jacob's reception upon returning home on September 26, 1900. The *Stonington Mirror* front-page article reporting this event is reprinted in its entirety below:

Jacob Welcomed

Over two hundred persons gathered near the old Steamboat hotel in the borough Wednesday evening to welcome Jacob Seidner on his return from abroad. Inside the house were many friends who had gathered to do him honor. Mr. Seidner arrived on the nine o'clock train and was at once escorted home amid the blaze of red fire and Roman candles and rockets, while the crowd cheered its welcome. A fine supper was enjoyed by the host and a few guests and speeches of welcome were made by prominent citizens.[192]

There is no mention of the family in this account, which may mean that Emma and the children returned home before Jacob, or it may simply be a reflection of the general dominance of men in society at the turn of the century.

BASED ON ARTICLES AND advertisements published in the *Stonington Mirror*, we know that Jacob had his shop and residence in the Steamboat Hotel from the summer of 1897 through at least October 1901, but eventually, he moved back to the main business district on Water Street. During this period, Jacob added a delicatessen and lunchroom to his tailor business, and once Jacob's son, Otto, was old enough to join the family business, he greatly expanded the delicatessen enterprise.

Jacob Seidner and his three children in front of his Water Street shop in Stonington. *Left to right*: Jacob, Olga, Otto and Sophie, probably between 1910 and 1914. The children's positions match their future careers. Olga and her husband would go on to run the family clothing business, and both Otto and Sophie, seen here in front of the lunch room, ran the family delicatessen and food manufacturing businesses. *Courtesy of Westerly Public Library and Wilcox Park.*

A photo of Jacob and his children taken in front of his shop on Water Street sometime between 1910 and 1914 shows signs for both "J. SEIDNER merchant and tailor" and "J. SEIDNER LUNCH ROOM German and French Delicates." The entrance to the Cassedy House hotel can be seen on the far right, offering "Board and Rooms."

IN 1910, ACCORDING TO the U.S. Census, Jacob and Emma Seidner were living on Water Street above their shop, with Olga (twenty), Sophie (eighteen) and Otto (sixteen), as well as a salesman, Harry Polonsky (twenty), who had emigrated from Russia. But by 1914, the family was living in a frame house on the corner of Grand and Gold Streets, a block from the Steamboat Hotel

The Seidner Block—constructed from bricks salvaged from the railroad roundhouse—as it appears today. Gold Street is in the foreground, and Grand Street is to the left. The building is an apartment complex today. *Author photo.*

and very near the railroad yard. Legend has it that, ever since his experiences with fire in the Steamboat Hotel, Jacob preferred not live in wood structures, and an opportunity to act on that preference eventually came his way.

Passenger steamboat and rail service through Stonington Harbor ended soon after the beginning of the new century, and all railroad activity in the center of the borough was abandoned by 1913. However, the New York, New Haven and Hartford railroad was slow to remove the tracks and buildings it left behind. The borough residents had hoped the tracks would be pulled up in time for the centennial celebration of the Battle of Stonington in August 1914, but that did not happen.[193]

The first structure the railroad finally took away was the engine roundhouse, and Jacob Seidner arranged to purchase the one hundred thousand bricks used to build it with the idea of constructing a brick structure for his family to live in.[194] According to a story I heard in town, Jacob paid neighbor children to knock the old mortar off the roundhouse bricks.[195] The original plan was for a three-story building, but the final structure—finished the same year—was a two-story building called the Seidner Block. Today the Seidner Block still stands on the corner of Grand and Gold, exactly one block south of the former Steamboat Hotel building.

A SOMEWHAT MYSTERIOUS EPISODE played out in the pages of the *Norwich Bulletin* newspaper in the spring of 1914. Norwich, Connecticut, is approximately twenty miles northwest of Stonington Borough, and the *Bulletin* regularly reported news from Stonington and Mystic. On March 31, the "About the Borough" section on page 2 included this short item: "Jacob Seidner has announced the engagement of his daughter Olga to Abraham Tannenbaum of New York." But three days later, a follow-up item appeared in the paper: "Contradict Report. Mr. and Mrs. Jacob Seidner deny the report of the engagement of their daughter, Miss Olga, to Abraham Tannenbaum of New York."[196] The reader is left to speculate about who Mr. Tannenbaum might have been and the story behind this episode.

Two years later, Olga Seidner did get married. In August 1916, she was wed to Henry Friedman of Newark, New Jersey, in a private ceremony at her parents' home. Despite Olga's Jewish heritage, the marriage was officiated by the pastor of a Congregational church in Bridgeport, Connecticut. According to the report in the *Mirror*, after a two-week honeymoon in Maine, the couple occupied "one of the tenements in the Seidner building," and Henry joined his father-in-law's business.[197]

SADLY, JACOB DID NOT have long to enjoy his new building or his daughter's marriage. Just before noon on April 25, 1917, while standing in the doorway of his house in conversation with his son-in-law, Jacob Seidner had a heart attack and died at the age of fifty-eight. The community was shocked by the sudden death of a man the *Mirror* described as "a well known and highly respected resident of Stonington."[198] There was a funeral service in the borough, but according to his wishes, Jacob's remains were transported to New York for cremation.

Emma Seidner lived another quarter of a century after her husband died but never remarried. She moved in with her unmarried daughter, Sophie, and died in their home on Moss Street in the Pawcatuck neighborhood of Stonington—just a few doors down from Otto and his family—on August 22, 1942, at the age of seventy-eight.

BY THE TIME OF Jacob's death, he and Otto had expanded the family business to include delicatessens in the neighboring towns of Mystic, Connecticut, and Westerly, Rhode Island, and Otto went on to be one of the area's most successful businessmen. In addition to the delicatessen stores, he was famous for his very popular Seidner's Mayonnaise, which he manufactured in a

An undated photo of a Seidner's mayonnaise truck. *Courtesy of the Westerly Public Library and Wilcox Park.*

factory in Westerly and shipped nationwide. Admiral Robert Byrd carried Seidner's Mayonnaise on his 1933 expedition to the South Pole because he believed it provided high nutritional value.[199] Otto married Lillian Block of New York, and they had two children, Arnold and Muriel. Otto was an avid yachtsman and deep-sea fisherman and a founder of the Westerly Yacht Club, as well as a generous philanthropist with a particular commitment to the Boy and Girl Scouts. During World War II, Otto lent his yacht *Muriel* to the United States Coast Guard, and when it was returned to him after the war, he received letters of commendation from both the Coast Guard and the navy.[200]

Otto eventually moved to the wealthy Watch Hill neighborhood of Westerly. Lillian died in 1966 at the age of seventy-four, and Otto remarried Gertrude Schwartz Silverman. He retired from his business in 1970 and died in 1973 at the age of seventy-nine. His passing was noted by several area papers, and the *Hartford Courant* called him "the Mayonnaise King." Otto and his first wife, Lillian, were buried together in the Beth El Cemetery in Providence, Rhode Island.

FOR MANY YEARS, HENRY Friedman followed in his father-in-law's business, operating Friedman's clothing store at the same location, 141 Water Street in the borough. He and Olga had one child, Arthur Jacob Friedman.

The third generation. *Left to right*: Arnold Seidner, Muriel Seidner and Arthur Friedman. The photo was probably taken in the early to mid-1930s. *Courtesy of the Westerly Public Library and Wilcox Park.*

Although Jacob's second daughter, Sophie, never married, she lived with her widowed mother in the Pawcatuck neighborhood of Stonington and ran the Westerly delicatessen. Mother and daughter often traveled together. On November 7, 1920, the *Norwich Bulletin* reported that Emma and Sophie were on vacation in Belgium and were expected to return home in December, and in March 1931, the women visited Havana, Cuba.

After Emma's death, Sophie often traveled with her older sister, Olga. In January 1947, Olga Friedman wrote a letter to the *Mirror-Journal* reporting a particularly noteworthy encounter. While visiting the Dunhill store on Fifth Avenue in New York, the sisters spotted the Duke of Windsor. "I made up my mind to speak to him, and I am sure glad I did, as he was very pleasant and I was certainly surprised to find him so easy to talk to," wrote Olga. She made no mention of the Duchess of Windsor, Wallis Simpson.

THE THIRD-GENERATION DESCENDANTS OF the immigrant tailor more than achieved the American Dream. Both of Jacob's male grandchildren attended Yale University. Olga's son, Arthur, graduated from Stonington High School, where he thrived, making honor roll all four years and participating in many clubs and activities. At Yale, he majored in economics, graduating in 1941, after which he enlisted in the Coast Guard, stationed first in Boston and later at the Coast Guard Academy in New London, Connecticut.

An undated springtime picture of teenaged Muriel Seidner. *Courtesy of the Westerly Public Library and Wilcox Park.*

Otto's business success allowed him to send Arnold and Muriel to boarding schools, and after graduation from Choate Rosemary Hall, Arnold studied international relations at Yale as a member of the class of '44. He left Yale during his senior year to serve in the navy during World War II, returning to graduate in January 1947. After graduation, he went home to help his father with the mayonnaise business.

Neither Yale nor Wesleyan accepted women at the time Muriel would have been eligible to attend. They would not do so until 1969 and 1970, respectively. After graduation from

Dana Hall School in Wellesley, Massachusetts, Muriel went to Rhode Island State College—now the University of Rhode Island—to study education. She achieved a 1950s female version of the American Dream by marrying a dentist—and not just any dentist but Dr. Irving Glickman, professor of dentistry at Tufts University.[201]

Although the Seidner-Friedman family had roots in southern New England, California tugged at them, and as many of them moved west, their trails go cold. Arthur Friedman left just a few breadcrumbs. He married a woman named Gertrude, and they lived out their lives in the Los Angeles area, finally in Pacific Palisades. Legal records show they entered into a limited partnership in 2000, perhaps for estate planning purposes, and dissolved it two years later.[202] Gertrude died in 2004 and Arthur died in 2006.

Arthur's parents also moved to the Los Angeles area, perhaps to retire close to their son. Olga and Henry Friedman lived in Seal Beach, California, east of downtown Los Angeles, and they are both buried in Westminster Memorial Park, in Orange County, California.

Muriel's marriage to Irving Glickman did not last long, and she came home to Rhode Island for a time and worked as a teacher. During this period, she went on a fishing trip off Acapulco, Mexico, where, continuing her father's passion for deep-sea fishing, she managed to catch a sailfish so large that a picture was carried in the January 10, 1954 edition of the *Boston Globe*. In the photo, Muriel can be seen smiling broadly with her pole in one hand. The nine-foot, ten-inch, 104-pound fish hangs by its tail next to her dwarfed frame. It took Muriel thirty-three minutes to bring in her catch using an eighteen-pound test line on a six-ounce rod.[203]

At some point, Muriel moved to California and in 1965 married Vernon M. Dove. Although this marriage lasted longer than her first, it also ended in divorce eight years later. After that, we lose track of her, but we know that she was living as Muriel Dove in Marina Del Ray, California, in 1985.

Of the three members of the third generation of the Seidner-Friedman family, we know the most about Arnold Seidner. After the war and graduation from Yale, he came home to work with his father, but he appears to have had a fascination with movie actresses.

Constance Cavendish-Hinckesman grew up in Vancouver, British Columbia, and in her early years, she began to gain attention as a talented dancer under the simplified name Constance Cavendish. After her family moved to California,

Constance Cavendish as "Gert 'the Bread' Evans" in the *Outer Limits* television episode "The Sixth Finger," which first aired on October 14, 1963. *Villa DiStefano Productions. Author collection.*

she danced with the Ballet Russe and the Los Angeles Civic Light Opera and had her Hollywood Bowl solo debut at the age of eighteen. Unfortunately, a serious accident left her paralyzed for two years and effectively ended her dancing career, but she came back as an actor. In 1948, she was a contestant on Don Ameche's talent quest radio show, *Your Lucky Strike,* and her performance led to a small nonspeaking role as Alice Forsyte in *That Forsyte Woman,* starring Errol Flynn, Greer Garson and Walter Pigeon. Although she was rarely a star, other movie, television and theater roles followed.

But before all this happened, Constance was volunteering as a waitress at the milk bar of the Servicemen's Canteen in Hollywood shortly after V-J Day in 1945. She broke the rule against dating servicemen only because Arnold Seidner threatened to keep drinking milk until he burst unless she agreed to go on a date with him. The two maintained a long-distance relationship for several years until Arnold took a break from working at the Seidner plant and returned to California with two goals: getting a master's degree at UCLA and marrying Constance.[204] He succeeded at both; however, like his

Wedding photo of Arnold Seidner and Constance Cavendish. *Courtesy of the Westerly Public Library and Wilcox Park.*

sister, Arnold was unlucky in love. The marriage was short-lived—perhaps because husband and wife were tied to opposite coasts.

SEIDNER'S MAYONNAISE IS NO longer on the market, and the reason appears to be that no one in the family wanted to take on the responsibility of keeping the business going. Soon after Otto Seidner retired and died, the company was sold to a firm in Providence, Rhode Island, that kept the mayonnaise available locally for a time.[205] But for reasons that are unclear, Arnold Seidner spent the last phase of his life in San Francisco, California.

Late in life, Arnold Seidner married his second movie actress, Polish stage and film star Barbara Krafftówna. Krafftówna was an accomplished Polish entertainer. By the time she and Arnold met, she had starred in twenty films and countless plays. In 1982, she immigrated to the United States, where she met Arnold, and the couple were married on December 16, 1984, when she was fifty-six and he was sixty-two. Barbara's first husband, the actor Michael Gazda, died in a car accident in 1969, and as a result, this was a second marriage for both.[206]

Sadly, the marriage lasted only four months because Arnold Seidner died of a heart attack on April 24, 1985, at the age of sixty-two. The brief obituary in the *San Francisco Examiner* did not mention his business career, but it listed his educational history, military service and membership in the San Francisco Press Club. Perhaps Arnold's most important civic function at the time of his death was as a member of the Board of Directors of the International Institute of San Francisco.

The International Institute movement began in 1910 in New York City as a program of the Young Women's Christian Association designed to provide newly arrived and first-generation immigrant girls and women with language classes, recreational activities and employment assistance.[207] International Institutes spread to other industrialized cities where there were significant numbers of immigrants, and the national organization eventually separated from the YWCA and widened its focus to immigrant families and immigrant communities as a whole.

Arnold Seidner had majored in international relations at Yale, and at the end of his life, this grandson of two Austrian immigrants was working to support other new arrivals to the United States. The International Institute of San Francisco continues today as the International Institute of the Bay Area. A World War II navy veteran, Arnold was buried in San Francisco National Cemetery in the Presidio of San Francisco.

Barbara Krafftówna in *Jak byc kochana* (*How to Be Loved*), 1963. *WFF Wroclaw.*

In the 1980s, the International Institute of San Francisco was assisting a wave of Polish refugees fleeing the disruption of the Solidarity movement,[208] and this political context may have led Barbara Krafftówna to meet Arnold Seidner. Barbara obtained U.S. citizenship, but in 1998, she returned to live permanently in Poland. She continued to act in films, television and on stage until 2017. On November 11, 2019, she was awarded the Commander's Cross with the Star of the Order of Polonia Restituta, the second-highest Polish civilian state decoration.[209] Krafftówna died on January 23, 2022, at the age of ninety-three. In a letter that was read at her funeral, Polish president Andrzej Duda wrote, "She was an artist of a huge and versatile talent, reinforced by great diligence and passion."[210] None of the obituaries made mention of her brief marriage to Arnold Seidner.

CHAPTER 11

THE CURTAIN CLOSES

W hen the roof of the Steamboat Hotel caught fire on the evening of May 24, 1899, in addition to Jacob Seidner's home and business, the building held rooms rented by the Arion Singing Society, an indirect product of industrialization. Since the mid-nineteenth century, the Atwood Machine Company, a maker of machine parts used in the silk industry, had operated a factory in the borough, but in the early 1890s, the American Velvet Company built a mill on a large plot of land within the boundaries of the borough but east of the peninsula. The opening of the velvet mill brought an influx of German immigrants to town, many of whom spoke only German, and the Arion Singing Society emerged as a social and cultural group for these workers.

At first, the group met in the homes of its members, but eventually it took rooms in the Steamboat Hotel. The society grew quickly, two years later moving to a larger space across the street in the Potter Block, and in November 1909 the society opened its own music hall—a two-story building with a full basement—on Cutler Street.[211] This final home could hold an audience of 150 and had a billiard hall on the first floor and two bowling lanes in the basement. The Arion Society held concerts and dances on a regular basis in various locations in the borough and provided music for special events. At the height of their activity, they sponsored an annual masquerade ball at their Cutler Street facility.

Just like many at the Steamboat Hotel before them, the Arion Singing Society ran afoul of the local liquor enforcement authorities, but only after they had moved across the street to the Potter Block. As the society grew, they founded the Columbian Orchestra, with Henry Engels as its leader and piano player. But on Friday, January 25, 1901, the Arion Society rooms in the Potter Block were raided by Sheriff J.H. Tubbs, and Henry Engels was arrested on the charge of selling "spiritous and intoxicating liquors."

The *Mirror*'s coverage of this incident and the subsequent trial was very sympathetic to the defendant: "The arrest has caused much indignation among the borough people, as the Arion Society is composed of all German residents who are substantial citizens of the place, the prisoner being a young man of exceptional character and is very popular."[212] The paper also reported that it was rumored that Henry would have a jury trial in the town court.[213]

The case was heard on February 4, in front of a packed courtroom. The proceedings went on for almost the entire afternoon, but according to the account in the *Mirror*, the prosecutor was unable to prove his case. When he asked for an adjournment, the court refused, and before five o'clock the prisoner was declared not guilty and released. "Herbert W. Rathburn appeared for the accused, and his skillful handling of the case pleased the audience. Much gratification is felt by friends of Mr. Engels."[214]

In 1912, Henry, with a partner, applied for a license to sell "spiritous and intoxicating liquors" on the ground floor of the Steamboat Hotel.[215] After several dry years in a row, the license contingent won by 201 votes that year. A year later, Engel and his partner installed a pool table in the saloon,[216] but in 1914, after two wet years, the town voted not to license liquor sales, forcing Engels and his partner to close the saloon.[217] Immediately thereafter, William and Margaret Foley's son, John A. Foley, announced plans to open a pool hall in the space previously occupied by Henry Engels's saloon.

ON DECEMBER 9, 1896, Ellen Foley died in a fire at her home on Granite Street in Westerly, Rhode Island. The two-story building was discovered fully engulfed at approximately one o'clock in the morning, and the evidence suggested that Mrs. Foley had been awakened in her second-floor bedroom and tried unsuccessfully to escape.[218] Following her death, ownership of the Steamboat Hotel fell to her eldest son, William Foley, who, like his father, worked as a stonecutter in the granite quarries of Westerly. In September 1921, William's wife, Margaret, sold the Steamboat Hotel building to William F. Loudon, a cement contractor from the Pawcatuck neighborhood of Stonington.

WILLIAM LOUDON WAS A successful entrepreneur who had a variety of businesses. Born in Norwalk, Connecticut, he came to the Westerly-Pawcatuck area in the early 1880s, where his first business venture was a fruit stand on Main Street in Westerly. In 1890, he founded the Westerly Concrete Company, which would become his primary business, specializing in paving sidewalks. Loudon was also a developer. He lived much of his life on Liberty Street in the Pawcatuck neighborhood of Stonington, and he bought and developed a tract of land just to the west of Liberty Street, creating streets and lots for home sites. The area was soon populated with modest homes and remains a vibrant neighborhood today. One of the roads created in the development was Loudon Avenue.[219]

William Loudon must have been a rather clever man, because in March 1902, he filed a U.S. patent for a new design of kerosene lamp constructed so that "the globe there of can be readily placed in position or removed there from and be held firmly in position and prevented from rattling while the lamp is in use."[220] Loudon's patent was granted on September 8, 1903, three days after his fortieth birthday, but there is no evidence that he ever produced or marketed the lamp.

In May 1883, William married Jennette Cartwright of Stonington at Christ Church Episcopal in Westerly, Rhode Island. The couple produced two children, Abel, born in 1884, and Carrie, born in 1887. Both Loudon children went on to marry and produce families of their own. In the 1920s, William Loudon began to shift his businesses away from concrete and development and toward real estate holdings and service businesses. He purchased a small hotel building on West Broad Street in Pawcatuck that became known as the Loudon Inn, and he and Jeanette moved there from Liberty Street to live in and operate the inn. Soon after, Loudon purchased the Steamboat Hotel, and in 1930, he retired from his concrete and land development businesses. His main retirement occupation was innkeeper, but after Prohibition ended, he also had a liquor store on Liberty Street.

William Loudon owned the Steamboat Hotel in the 1920s, and in 1925, he bought the Potter Block and rented out space in it to serve as the borough post office. There is little evidence of retail activity in the Steamboat Hotel in the 1920s, but we know that John Lopes, a popular immigrant from the Azores Islands, operated a barbershop in the building because on November 13, 1925, the police raided the shop and uncovered a small amount of liquor in a five-gallon can. Lopes was freed on $2,000 bond and appeared in court the next morning, where Judge William A. Wilcox sentenced him to a $75 fine and $27.06 in court costs.[221]

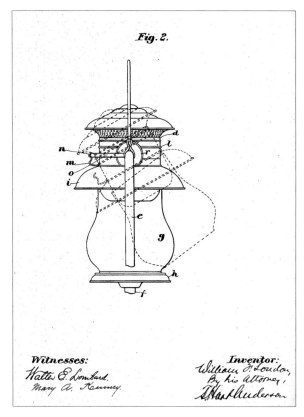

Left: An illustration filed with William F. Loudon's 1902 patent application for a new kerosene lamp design. *U.S. Patent No. 738,689, September 8, 1903.*

Below: A 1931 postcard photo of the Loudon Inn on West Broad Street in the Pawcatuck neighborhood of Stonington, Connecticut (incorrectly identified as Westerly, Rhode Island). William Loudon ran the inn and lived there with his wife. *Author's collection.*

William Loudon died at his home in the Loudon Inn on September 19, 1947, at the age of eighty-four. He had been predeceased by both his wife, Jeannette, and his son, Abel, but at the time of his death he was survived by his daughter, Carrie Loudon Stillman, twelve grandchildren and four great-grandchildren. His obituary in the *Westerly Sun* called him "a pioneer in the construction of sidewalks, not only in this section but in Waterbury, Norwalk, and other Connecticut cities." He was remembered as an avid harness racer, whose pacer Smoky was particularly fast on snow and ice, and for his interest in community affairs. He once served as sealer of weights and measures in Stonington.

AS THEY AGE, HOTELS realize a number of possible fates. Some continue on as hotels. The Biltmore in Providence, where David Hall worked and died, remains a fine facility, now called the Graduate Providence. The Biltmore fell on hard times and closed in 1975, lying vacant for four years, but Providence mayor Vincent "Buddy" Cianci worked to have the building designated a landmark on the National Register of Historic Places and assembled a group of businesspeople to buy and renovate the building. The hotel has had various owners over the years, but all have retained the iconic Biltmore sign on the roof of the building. The year 2022 marked a century since David Hall, newly called out of retirement, helped open the Biltmore Hotel.

Other hotels burn down or are demolished. The City Hotel in New London, the Ocean House in Newport and the Aldrich House in Providence—all places where W. Frank Hall worked—were destroyed by fire. In fact, the Ocean House burned to the ground twice. Stonington's most grand hotel, the Wadawanuck, was taken apart and used to build or repair several homes in the borough, and Providence's Narraganset Hotel, where David Hall was proprietor at the peak of his career, was torn down to make way for a parking garage.

Hotels that cease to be hotels yet avoid demolition tend to become apartment or condominium buildings. This has been the fate of the Updike House in East Greenwich, Rhode Island, where Dorcas Hall spent her final years, and the Martin House in Westerly, Rhode Island, built by Michael and Mary Martin, as well as Stonington's Cassedy House and Ocean House hotels. All four buildings now have apartments or condominiums on the upper floors and commercial spaces on the first floor.

This has also been the fate of Stonington's Steamboat Hotel. For a time, the retail spaces on the first floor were occupied by various businesses and organizations, but without steamboats or trains to provide east–west foot traffic on Pearl Street, the first-floor retail spaces were eventually converted into additional apartments. In the early decades of the twentieth century, any article in the *Mirror-Journal* that mentioned the building was likely to call it "the old Steamboat Hotel." Eventually, with Stonington's steamboat era long past, the name was changed first to the Harbor View Inn and finally to the Harbor View Apartments. The mix of public and private dramas characteristic of a hotel building had become merely private ones playing out behind closed doors, and as a result, the curtain fell on this history.

EPILOGUE

W hen you live in a place, its dimensions and outlines gradually come into view. You learn how to get from here to there. You become familiar with the geography and the changing seasons and light. You experience its celebrations and its tragedies. You get to know the shopkeepers, your neighbors and your neighbors' dogs.

Long before the coronavirus pandemic came to town and I began writing about the Steamboat Hotel, this was all true of me. I had a rich community life in Stonington, made possible by spending time in the company of the people of this place. I was perfectly happy, and becoming a historian was far from my mind. But then a fragment of a story came to light during the early days of my coronavirus quarantine, and when I looked up a few months later, I was writing this history.

I have written a few other books before, but this one is different. This one was written out of love, the love of a beautiful spit of land in southeastern New England and the people who live there. This book is a gift to that place and to those people, but in giving it, I have received much in return. Everything in Stonington Borough is the same as when I started this project, but for me, everything has changed. The people of this story have all come alive for me in a way that will make the rest of my time in this village a richer and more resonant experience.

When I look west from my rooms in the old Steamboat Hotel building, I see the harbor as it has always been, but now I also see stately steamboats puffing toward the piers, filled with passengers scurrying to gather up their belongings in preparation to disembark for waiting trains. I can also see the breakwater where summer sunbathers once spread their towels on the rocks and where couples cuddled together. To the south, I see the railroad roundhouse bricks that now form the Seidner Block, where Jacob Seidner and his family lived. A little to the east, I see Water Street, where Jacob Seidner had his tailor shop and delicatessen, and I see the roofs of the former Cassedy House and Ocean House hotels. Just across Pearl Street to the north, I look out on the Müller Block that was scaled by the human fly Johnny J. Woods in 1931 and 1947 and where, beginning in the late nineteenth century, August Müller and his descendants sold furniture. I can also see the Potter Block, where the Arion Singing Society rented rooms, where Henry Engel was arrested for illegal liquor sales and where Jacob Seidner rushed into flames and smoke in a brave attempt to save a baker.

On my walks through town, I pass the spot where the Wadawanuck Hotel once stood and the corner of Main and Wall Streets, where the Amos Palmer House, home to the George Whistler and Stephen Vincent Binet families, still stands. Just to the east, I can walk down Wall Street, passing by the spot where W. Henry Wood, a much-respected constable, and Ashea Barnswell Wood, the daughter of a New York restaurant family, made their home and raised their children.

In the middle of it all, there is the shadow of a cut, the remnants of railroad tracks that entered from the east side of town, slicing through the middle of the peninsula to the harbor on the west. Today, buildings have grown up over much of the track bed, but next to the old Congregational church and at points east, a grassy graded streak between the houses is enough to evoke the memory of Major George Wheeler, David Crowley, Daniel Webster, Margaret Barnswell and the many others who came to a small village in Connecticut on clouds of steam.

My life in this village will never be quite the same. I know many more people in town than I did when I started this project. That all of them were dead long before I came to know them is of little consequence. Often, we live our lives stuck in the present, as though things were always as they are in this moment. But it can be an instructive joy to be awakened from our myopic dreams and remember that others walked these streets before us, selling their wares, providing needed services, enjoying their entertainments and building families. It was not always thus, and with their small individual efforts, the people who came before us helped build a way of life, a community and a nation. Somewhat by accident, I have experienced that instructive joy while writing this book, and for that happy accident, I will be forever grateful.

ACKNOWLEDGEMENTS

This book is dedicated to the memory of two men with strong connections to Stonington Borough. Anthony Bailey was a British expatriate and staff writer for the *New Yorker* magazine for more than three decades. In part because he was an avid sailor, he lived in Stonington Borough for many years with his wife and four daughters. In 1971, he published *In the Village*, an evocative love letter to life in our little community. He moved back to England not long after *In the Village* was published, and in May 2020, as I was starting to work on this project, word came that Bailey had contracted COVID-19 and died while in the hospital recovering from hip surgery.[222] *In the Village* was an important influence on this project, and I was delighted to hear that the Stonington Historical Society plans to publish a new edition of the book, making this literary gem available to new generations of readers.

Jack Fix was an artist, teacher and loyal friend to Stonington. There are few people who have volunteered more time to more organizations in the borough than Jack. Although I worked with him in two other civic organizations in Stonington, I didn't know that Jack had any connection to the Stonington Historical Society. As I began to work with photographs and other documents in the historical society's collection, I discovered that, more often than not, the item I was looking at had been carefully cataloged and filed by Jack Fix. It seems only appropriate to dedicate this book to his memory in appreciation of all he was and did.

No one would accuse me of being a historian. I am a psychologist, an academic and a science writer. When I took on this project, I had never done the kind of serious detective work required to uncover and reconstruct a historical record. As a result, I could not have produced this story of the Steamboat Hotel but for the generosity of several Stonington historians who are far more knowledgeable than I. I had enormous assistance from Chelsea Mitchell of the Stonington Historical Society, Mary M. Thacher, Bob Suppicich and Larry O'Keefe. In particular, long before I became interested in the Steamboat Hotel, my Gold Street neighbor, Mary Thacher, had already done a title search of the building and written a fascinating document entitled "Baptists, Temperance, and the Steamboat Hotel," much of which found its way into this volume. We soon struck up a collaboration, and I became apprenticed to her in the mysterious arts of plumbing Ancestry.com, FindaGrave.com and the archives of various state and municipal offices. She also read every chapter and provided essential feedback. Mary has been an enormously valuable—and fun—mentor, and I am very grateful to her. I owe a particular debt to people who read part or all of the manuscript, including James Longenbach, Harry Martin, Chelsea Mitchell, Joanna Scott, Mary Thacher, Christine Turentine and Elizabeth Wood. Others who have provided useful counsel include my friends Simon Feldman, Jerry Fischer, Lynn Callahan and Christopher Steiner. Ashlynn Rickord, director of city cemeteries for the city of Providence, Rhode Island, and the staff of the Rhode Island Historical Society provided invaluable documents and leads, as did Thomas Kramer of the New London Public Library. Finally, it has been a pleasure to work with editors Michael G. Kinsella and Zoe Ames of The History Press.

This book would not have been possible without newspapers. In particular, had the *Stonington Mirror* not existed and or not been preserved, a priceless historical resource would be lost. I was greatly aided by the use of searchable online editions of several newspapers, including the *Stonington Mirror* (later the *Stonington Mirror and Mystic Journal*), the *Nantucket Inquirer and Mirror* (which can be accessed online for free), the *Brooklyn Daily Eagle*, the *New York Times* and the *Boston Daily Globe*. In addition, much of this history played out in small places: Stonington Village and Nantucket Island, communities where everyone was known and the smallest events made their way into the pages of the local paper. These fortunate circumstances made my job much easier.

There have been some wonderful strokes of luck. One of these was the discovery of a beautiful portrait of David Crowley, one of the most important characters in this story, in the collections of the Rhode Island Historical Society. Another was the discovery that Sarah Crowley Hemeon had the generosity and good sense to deposit several portraits from the Crowley-

Arnold family and other items with the Nantucket Historical Association. Another stroke of luck: Barnswell was an unusual name in the New York of the late nineteenth century, making it much easier to track this remarkable family. While I was working on this book, Jack Martin of Saverna Park, Maryland, who is related to Michael F. Martin, one of the proprietors of the Steamboat Hotel, was doing his own family research and contacted the Stonington Historical Society. Chelsea Mitchell put him in touch with me, and he provided some valuable details and was indirectly responsible for uncovering a previously unknown photo of the hotel. Through a DNA match, Jack found another relation, Lisa Specht Ackerman, who had the photo. Lisa generously donated the photo to the Stonington Historical Society. Finally, a distant relation of the Seidner family donated a large and very valuable collection of Seidner family documents to the Westerly Public Library and Wilcox Park. I would like to thank Nina Wright for her help with these materials.

All of these people and events came together to create this happy accident.

NOTES

Chapter 1

1. Norman J. Brouwer, *Steamboats on Long Island Sound* (Charleston, SC: Arcadia Publishing, 2014), 7.
2. Ronald Karr, *The Rail Lines of Southern New England*, 2nd ed. (Pepperel, MA: Branch Line Press, 2017), 177.
3. Brouwer, *Steamboats*.
4. George L. Vose, *A Sketch of the Life and Works of George W. Whistler Civil Engineer* (Boston: Lee and Shepard Publishers, 1887), 17–20.
5. Frank Heppner, *Railroads of Rhode Island: Shaping the Ocean State's Railways* (Charleston, SC: The History Press 2012), 24–25.
6. Initially, there was just a single dock. Later, a second steamboat dock was built just south of the original one.
7. Vose, *George W. Whistler*.
8. William Haynes, *Stonington Chronology 1649–1949: Being a Year-by-Year Record of the American Way of Life in a Connecticut Town* (Stonington, CT: Pequot Press, 1949), 45.
9. Vose, *George W. Whistler*.
10. Ibid.
11. This account of the events of November 10, 1837, C is drawn from Henry Robinson Palmer, *Stonington by the Sea*, 2nd ed. (Stonington, CT: Palmer Press, 1957; originally published 1913).

Chapter 2

12. Ibid.

13. Ibid.

14. Richard Anson Wheeler, *History of the Town of Stonington, County of New London, Connecticut, from Its First Settlement in 1649 to 1900* (New London, CT: Day Publishing, 1900), 652.

15. Emma Palmer, "Hotels and Taverns," Stonington (CT) Historical Society, n.d. A version of the story also appears in Palmer, *Stonington by the Sea.*

16. Mary Thacher, title search for "23 Gold Street," n.d.

17. There is some confusion about his first name. The surviving documents variously identify Mr. Capron as C.B., Gurnel, Cornel and Colonel. Absent any clear path, I have chosen to use Colonel.

18. Emma Palmer, "The Wadawanuck Hotel," *Mirror and Journal* (Stonington, CT), November 5, 1937.

19. Palmer, "Hotels and Taverns."

20. Palmer, "Wadawanuck Hotel."

21. Minor Myers Jr., "Wadawanuck Young Ladies Institute: Connecticut's First Women's College," *Historical Footnotes* 16, no. 1 (November 1978), 1–2, 6, 8, 10.

22. Haynes, *Stonington Chronology*, 75–77.

23. *Weekly Mirror Journal* (Stonington, CT), August 22, 1872.

24. *The Season: An Independent Critical Journal* 1, no. 12 (December 24, 1870): 100.

25. *The Season: An Independent Critical Journal* 2, no. 6 (February 11, 1871: 46.

26. Amy. "Blocked Out from Block Island," *Stonington (CT) Mirror,* October 3, 1872.

27. Haynes, *Stonington Chronology*, 68; Palmer, *Stonington by the Sea*, 51.

28. Palmer, *Stonington by the Sea.*

29. Haynes, *Stonington Chronology*, 87.

30. Palmer, "Hotels and Taverns."

31. *Mirror and Journal* (Stonington, CT), January 8, 1937; Austin Weber, "The History of Caskets," *Assembly*, October 2, 2009, https://www.assemblymag.com/articles/87043-the-history-of-caskets.

32. Jerome S. Anderson, *Anderson's Stonington (CT) Directory* (Stonington, CT: Jerome S. Anderson, 1881), 163.

33. *Stonington (CT) Mirror*, September 5, 1878.

34. *Stonington (CT) Mirror*, September 5, 1891.

35. *Stonington (CT) Mirror*, May 29, 1931.

36. This section on human flies owes much to Jacob Smith, *The Thrill Makers: Celebrity, Masculinity, and Stunt Performers* (Berkeley: University of California Press, 2012), 48–80.

37. "Many View 'Human Fly,'" *New Britain (CT) Daily Herald*, September 24, 1930; "Human Fly Grosses 500 for TB Drive," *Sunday Star-News* (Wilmington, NC), December 21, 1947.

38. *Stonington (CT) Mirror*, July 10, 1931.

39. "Human Fly Returns to Boro," *Mirror-Journal* (Stonington, CT), May 2, 1947.

Chapter 3

40. Roger Williams McAdam, *Salts of the Sound* (Brattleboro, VT: Stephen Daye Press, 1939), 32.

41. George H. Hilton, *The Night Boat* (Berkeley, CA: Howell-North Books, 1968), 62.

42. Fred Erving Dayton, *Steamboat Days* (New York: Frederick A. Stokes, 1925), 207.

43. McAdam, *Salts of the Sound*, 33.

44. Dayton, *Steamboat Days*.

45. Dayton, *Steamboat Days*.

46. *The Youth's Companion* 54, no. 10 (March 10, 1881): 87.

Chapter 4

47. Benjamin F. Thompson, *History of Long Island from Its Discovery and Settlement to the Present Time*, vol. 1 (New York: Robert H. Dodd, 1918).

48. Harry T. Peters, *Currier & Ives: Printmakers to the American People* (Garden City, NY: Doubleday, Doran, 1942), 1.

49. Claude Moore Guess, *Daniel Webster*, vol. 2. (Boston: Little, Brown, 1930), 82.

50. Haynes, *Stonington Chronology*, 62.

51. Palmer, "Hotels and Taverns."

52. Robert V. Remini, *Daniel Webster: The Man and His Time* (New York: W. W. Norton, 1997), 466.

53. Palmer, "Hotels and Taverns."

54. Grace Denison Wheeler, *The Homes of Our Ancestors in Stonington, Conn.* (Salem, MA: Newcomb & Gauss, Printers, 1903), 68.

55. Hilton, *Night Boat*, 75.

Chapter 5

56. "An Escape," *The Youth's Companion* 54, no. 10 (March 5, 1881).

57. David Crowley, letter to Captain John States, March 5, 1940. Stonington Historical Society.

58. Again, I am indebted to Mary M. Tacher, who obtained the divorce records for David and Dorcas Crowley.

59. Carl W. Hall, *A Biographical Dictionary of People in Engineering: From the Earliest Records Until 2000* (West Lafayette, IN: Purdue University Press, 2008), 102.

60. Mary M. Thacher, transcription of divorce petitions: *David Crowley v. Dorcas Crowley* and *Dorcas Crowley v. David Crowley*, April 1856. Connecticut State Library, Hartford, Connecticut.

61. "Alexander Lyman Holley," NYC Parks, accessed April 20, 2021, https://www.nycgovparks.org/parks/washington-square-park/monuments/735.

62. Betsy Tyler, "Hadwen House," in *Properties Guide* (Nantucket, MA: Nantucket Historical Society, 2015), 62–71.

63. *Inquirer and Mirror* (Nantucket, MA), January 4, 1879.

64. Nantucket Marriage Registry, 1899. Via Ancestry.com, Massachusetts, U.S., Town and Vital Records, 1620–1988 (database online).

65. "Crowley Brings Suit for $30,000," *Inquirer and Mirror* (Nantucket, MA), January 11, 1913.

66. "Funeral of Mrs. Crowley," *Inquirer and Mirror* (Nantucket, MA), January 11, 1913.

67. "Crowley Files Appeal," *Inquirer and Mirror* (Nantucket, MA), January 18, 1913.

68. "Crowley Appointed Guardian," *Inquirer and Mirror* (Nantucket, MA), March 8, 1913.

69. "Another Prize Dance," *Inquirer and Mirror* (Nantucket, MA), May 1, 1915.

70. "Death of C.H. Crowley," *Inquirer and Mirror* (Nantucket, MA), May 19, 1934.

71. "Narrow Escape from Drowning," *Inquirer and Mirror* (Nantucket, MA), February 16, 1918.

72. "Mr. Crowley's retirement," *Providence (RI) Daily Journal*, August 22, 1881.

73. *Providence (RI) Daily Journal*, August 22, 1881.

74. "One Child Killed," *Boston Daily Globe*, March 2, 1893.

75. Ibid. I have changed the format of these quotes, but they are complete and verbatim.

Chapter 6

76. Daniel Okrent, *Last Call: The Rise and Fall of Prohibition* (New York: Scribner, 2010), 7.

77. Ibid., 11–12.

78. Harry M. Cassidy, "Liquor Control in the United States," in *Editorial Research Reports 1928*, vol. 3 (Washington, D.C.: CQ Press, 1928), 685, http://library.cqpress.com/cqresearcher/cqresrre1928080700.

79. "An Act in Addition to an Act concerning Crimes and Punishments," in *Public Acts Passed by the General Assembly of the State of Connecticut* (Hartford: Case, Lockwood, and Brainard, Printers, 1872), 98–101.

80. "An Act in Addition to an Act for the Observance of the Sabbath or the Lord's Day," in *Public Acts Passed*.

81. Okrent, *Last Call*, 148.

82. Annemarie McAllister, "The Alternative World of the Proud Non-Drinker: Nineteenth-Century Public Displays of Temperance," *Social History of Alcohol and Drugs* 28, no. 2 (Summer 2014): 161–79.

83. Much of this section is indebted to a document by Mary Thacher called "Baptists, Temperance, and the Steamboat Hotel" (Stonington Historical Society, n.d.).

84. Haynes, *Stonington Chronology*, 74.

85. *Stonington (CT) Mirror*, April 6, 1871.

86. *Stonington (CT) Mirror*, October 14, 1875.

87. *Stonington (CT) Mirror*, July 6, 1871.

Chapter 7

88. Deborah Davis, *Gilded: How Newport Became America's Richest Resort* (Hoboken, NJ: Wiley, 2009), 12–13.

89. Jon Sterngass, *First Resorts: Pursuing Pleasure at Saratoga Springs, Newport, and Coney Island* (Baltimore, MD: Johns Hopkins Press, 2001), 40–42.

90. Sterngass, *First Resorts*, 45.

91. Bryant F. Tolles Jr., *Summer by the Seaside: The Architecture of New England Costal Resort Hotels, 1820–1950* (Hanover, NH: University Press of New England, 2008), 37–38.

92. Sterngass, *First Resorts*, 63.

93. Livia Gershon, "The Rebellious, Scandalous Origins of Polka," *JSTOR Daily*, February 10, 2020, https://daily.jstor.org/the-rebellious-scandalous-origins-of-polka/.

94. Johnna Kaplan, "Other Than That, Mr. Lincoln..." Patch, April 8, 2011, https://patch.com/connecticut/newlondon/other-than-that-mr-lincoln.

95. "Cronin Building (1892)." Historic Buildings of Connecticut, January 26, 2015, http://historicbuildingsct.com/cronin-building-1892/.

96. *Bristol (RI) Phoenix*, August 15, 1868; *Providence (RI) Daily Journal*, August 11, 1868.

97. David Brussat, *Lost Providence* (Charleston, SC: The History Press, 2017), 49.

98. Rhode Island Historical Preservation and Heritage Commission, May 9, 2012.

99. Moses King, *King's Pocketbook of Providence* (Cambridge, MA: Moses King, 1882), 54.

100. David Morton Stone, *Lost Restaurants of Providence* (Charleston, SC: The History Press, 2019).

101. *Newport (RI) Daily News*, January 24, 1913.

102. R.L. Wilson, *Buffalo Bill's Wild West: An American Legend* (New York: Random House, 1998), 13.

103. Brussat, *Lost Providence*, 49. It should be noted that Major League Baseball considers the 1903 World Series to be the first.

104. *Newport (RI) Mercury*, December 23, 1882.

105. 1880 U.S. Census, East Greenwich, Rhode Island.

106. Bruce MacGunnigle, "Historic Moments Witnessed at EG's Greenwich Hotel," *Independent* (Wakefield, RI), October 22, 2012, https://www.independentri.com/independents/north_east/east_greenwich/article_bfa1acbf-3f07-5991-a32f-02f6d088dcef.html.

107. *Stonington (CT) Mirror*, October 7, 1908.

108. "Jed Prouty Dead; Stage, Film Actor," *New York Times*, May 11, 1956, https://nyti.ms/3ozal6Z.

109. "Clarence Gordon Prouty," Familysearch.org, https://www.familysearch.org/ark:/61903/1:1:2436-4KP.

110. "Hits by Newcomers in This Summer Show," *New York Times*, June 14, 1910.

111. *New York Times*, November 1, 1914; "'Miss Springtime' Has Rich Melodies," *New York Times*, September 26, 1916, https://nyti.ms/3vnyCQc.

112. "Miss Springtime," Internet Broadway Database, https://www.ibdb.com/broadway-production/miss-springtime-8446#People.

113. "Movies Boom Liberty Loan," *New York Times*, September 19, 1917, https://nyti.ms/2Sr7D7K.

114. "Jed Prouty's Car Kills Boy," *Sun* (New York), September 30, 1919.

115. "Wife of David B. Hall Dead at New York City Hospital," *Providence (RI) Daily Journal*, January 26, 1920.

116. " Person Details," Rhode Island Historical Cemetery Commission," accessed May 26, 2021, http://rihistoriccemeteries.org/newgravedetails.aspx?ID=406470.

117. "Jed Prouty," IMDb, https://www.imdb.com/name/nm0698985/.

118. 1930 U.S. Census.

119. "The Show Is On—Cast," Playbill, https://www.playbill.com/personlistpage/person-list?production=00000150-aea6-d936-a7fd-eef6ed340003&type=op#oc.

120. "Marion Murray," IMDb, https://www.imdb.com/name/nm0615156/.

121. "David B. Hall, Dean of Hotel Men, Dead," *Providence (RI) Daily Journal*, January 19, 1926.

122. Robert L. Wheeler, "Now and Then," in *Providence (RI) Daily Journal*, n.d. Obtained from the Rhode Island Collection, Providence Public Library.

123. Tolles, *Summer by the Seaside*.

124. Brussat, *Lost Providence*, 49; Stone, *Lost Restaurants of Providence*.

Chapter 8

125. *Stonington (CT) Mirror*, November 5, 1870.

126. *Brooklyn (NY) Daily Eagle*, September 10, 1884.

127. *Stonington (CT) Mirror*, February 12, 1874.

128. *Stonington (CT) Mirror*, May 31, 1895.

129. *Stonington (CT) Mirror*, August 27, 1874.

130. The first Black student was Wilbur Fisk Burns, class of 1860, the son of the Liberian Methodist bishop. David B. Potts, *Wesleyan University, 1831–1910: Collegiate Enterprise in New England* (Hanover, NH: Wesleyan University Press, 1999), 55.

131. Robert Bruce Slater, "The Blacks Who First Entered the World of White Higher Education," *Journal of Blacks in Higher Education* 4 (summer 1994), 47–56.

132. Potts, *Wesleyan University*, 54.

133. Cited in Potts, *Wesleyan University*, 265.

134. *Alumni Record* (Middletown, CT: Wesleyan University, 1911), 194.

135. Anton-Hermann Chroust, "American Legal Profession: Its Agony and Ecstasy," *Notre Dame Law Review* 46, no. 3 (Spring 1971): 487–525.

136. *Stonington (CT) Mirror*, March 2, 1871.

137. *Alumni Record*, 194.

138. *Stonington (CT) Mirror*, June 7, 1977.

139. Clara Merritt DeBoer, *His Truth Is Marching On: African Americans Who Taught the Freemen for the American Missionary Association, 1861–1877* (New York: Garland Publishing, 1995).

140. Ibid., 229.

141. "Additional Claims for Damages," *New York Times*, August 5, 1863.

142. National Archives (Washington, D.C.), U.S. Freedmen's Bureau Records, 1865–1878. Records of the Field Offices for the State of Georgia, Bureau of Refugees, Freedmen, and Abandoned Lands, 1865–1872; series number: M1903; reel number: 29; record group number: 105; record group name: Records of the Bureau of Refugees, Freedmen, and Abandoned Lands, 1861–1880; collection title: United States Freedmen's Bureau Hospital and Medical Records 1865–1872.

143. Heather M. Butts, "Alexander Thomas Augusta—Physician, Teacher and Human Rights Activist," *Journal of the National Medical Association* 97, no. 1 (January 2005): 106–9; Gerald S. Henig, "The First Black Physician in the U.S. Army," *Army History* 2, no. 87 (Spring 2013): 23–31.

144. "Dr. Alexander Augusta," National Park Service, February 28, 2021, https://www.nps.gov/foth/learn/historyculture/alexander-augusta.htm.

145. This is a quote from Augusta's description of the incident as reported in Butts, "Alexander Thomas Augusta."

146. Butts, "Alexander Thomas Augusta," 29.

147. "Plessy v. Ferguson," Wikipedia.com, https://en.wikipedia.org/wiki/Plessy_v._Ferguson.

148. National Archives (Washington, D.C.), Records of the Field Offices for the State of Georgia, Bureau of Refugees, Freedmen, and Abandoned Lands, 1865–1872; series number: M1903; reel number: 21; record group number: 105; record group name: Records of the Bureau

of Refugees, Freedmen, and Abandoned Lands, 1861–1880; collection title: United States Freedmen's Bureau Records of Persons and Articles Hired 1865–1872.

149. Ibid.

150. Ibid.

151. "Dr. Alexander Augusta"; Jimmy Fenison, "Alexander T. Augusta (1825–1890)," Blackpast, March 29, 2009, https://www.blackpast.org/african-american-history/augusta-alexander-t-1825-1890/.

152. "Dr. Alexander Augusta."

153. Craig Steven Wilder, *In the Company of Black Men: The African Influence on African American Culture in New York City* (New York: NYU Press, 2005), 187.

154. U.S. Census, 1880, Brooklyn, Kings County, New York.

155. "Colored Citizens," *Brooklyn (NY) Daily Eagle*, October 15, 1881.

156. "Recognition: The Claims of Colored Republicans," *Brooklyn (NY) Daily Eagle*, April 16, 1884.

157. "Robbed at Coney Island: Mr. Barnswell's Unique Adventures After Night in the 'Gut,'" *Brooklyn (NY) Daily Eagle*, September 27, 1885.

158. "A Mother's Rights. Judge Cullen Is Quite Severe on a Colored Gentleman." *Brooklyn (NY) Daily Eagle*, January 13, 1886.

159. "He Sued His Landlord, but Lost the Civil as well as the Criminal Action," *Brooklyn (NY) Daily Eagle*, April 12, 1888, 10.

160. "All Knew 'Tom' Barnswell. Death of a Character Well Known in Brooklyn for Many Years," *Brooklyn (NY) Daily Eagle*, November 22, 1892, 12.

161. *Record and Guide* (New York), October 4, 1884, https://rerecord.library.columbia.edu/pdf_files/ldpd_7031128_034_14.pdf.

162. Haynes, *Stonington Chronology*, 86.

Chapter 9

163. John Hill, "Westerly Granite Found in Hundreds of Statues, from Gettysburg to Roger Williams Statue," *Providence (RI) Journal*, October 6, 2013.

164. Thomas Williams Bicknell, *The History of the State of Rhode Island and Providence Plantations*, vol. 8 (New York: American Historical Society, 1920), 178–79.

165. David F. Musto, "Alcohol in American History," *Scientific American* 274, no. 4 (1996): 78–83.

166. *Stonington (CT) Mirror*, April 17, 1879.

167. *Stonington (CT) Mirror*, January 20, 1883.

168. Victor A. Rapport, "The Growth and Changing Functions of the Connecticut Department of State Police," *Journal of Criminal Law and Criminology* 30, no. 3 (1939), 359–69.

169. Henry William Blair, *The Temperance Movement or the Conflict between Man and Alcohol* (Boston: William E. Smythe, 1888), 32.

170. Rapport, "Growth and Changing Functions," 362.

171. *Stonington (CT) Mirror*, March 17, 1883.

172. *Stonington (CT) Mirror*, March 24, 1883.

173. *Stonington (CT) Mirror*, October 3, 1883.

174. *Stonington (CT) Mirror and Mystic Journal*, May 27, 1937.

175. Haynes, *Stonington Chronology*, 85.

176. *Stonington (CT) Mirror*, October 22, 1892.

177. S.E. Williams, "The Use of Beverage Alcohol as Medicine, 1790–1860," *Journal of Studies on Alcohol* 41, no. 5 (1980): 543–66.

178. Okrent, *Last Call*, 194.

179. Ibid., 196.

180. *Stonington (CT) Mirror*, April 18, 1891.

181. *Stonington (CT) Mirror*, June 18, 1892.

182. *Stonington (CT) Mirror*, October 28, 1893.

183. Bicknell, *State of Rhode Island*, 178–79.

184. *Westerly (RI) Sun*, February 23, 1939.

Chapter 10

185. *Stonington (CT) Mirror*, June 11, 1897.

186. "Bravery Rewarded," *Stonington (CT) Mirror*, March 18, 1898.

187. "Borough Blaze. Roof of the Old Steamboat Hotel Building Slightly Burned," *Stonington Mirror*, May 26, 1899.

188. Haynes, *Stonington Chronology*, 91.

189. "New London," Encyclopedia.com, https://www.encyclopedia.com/religion/encyclopedias-almanacs-transcripts-and-maps/new-london.

190. Brad Benson, *Village of the Soul: The Life of a Jewish Community*, 2004, https://www.congregationsharahzedek.org/wp-content/uploads/2020/12/jewisharticle.pdf.

191. Marian L. Smith, "Any Woman Who Is Now or May Hereafter Be Married…," *Prologue Magazine* 30, no. 2 (Summer 1998), https://www.

archives.gov/publications/prologue/1998/summer/women-and-naturalization-1.html.

192. "Jacob Welcomed," *Stonington (CT) Mirror,* September 28, 1900.

193. Robert Suppicich, personal communication with the author, 2021.

194. "Tearing Down Old Roundhouse," *Norwich (CT) Bulletin,* July 18, 1914.

195. This story was told to me by the building's current owners, Tucker and Sandy Bragdon.

196. "Contradict Report," *Norwich Stonington (CT) Bulletin,* April 3, 1914.

197. "Friedman-Seidner," *Stonington (CT) Mirror,* September 7, 1916.

198. "Sudden Death of Jacob Seidner," *Stonington (CT) Mirror,* April 26, 1917.

199. "'Mayonnaise King' Dead at 79," *Hartford (CT) Courant,* October 3, 1973.

200. These letters are held by the Westerly (Rhode Island) Library and Wilcox Park.

201. "Dr. Irving Glickman to Mary Miss Muriel Seidner in Fall," *Boston Globe,* July 13, 1952.

202. "Arthur and Gertrude Friedman Limited Partnership," OpenCorporates, https://opencorporates.com/filings/378851907.

203. *Boston Globe,* January 10, 1954.

204. All of this material about Constance Cavendish comes from Bob Willett, "The Girl Who Came Back," *Vancouver (BC) Sun,* December 15, 1951.

205. "Mr. Seidner Dies at 79."

206. "Barbara Krafftówna," Wikipedia, https://pl.wikipedia.org/wiki/Barbara_Krafftówna.

207. Raymond A. Mohl, "The International Institute Movement and Ethnic Pluralism" *Social Science* 56, no. 1 (1981): 14–21.

208. "IIBA's 104-Year History," Immigration Institute of the Bay Area, https://iibayarea.org/about/history/.

209. "Barbara Krafftówna."

210. "Last Farewell to Distinguished Actress Barbara Krafftówna," TVN24 News in English, February 4, 2022, https://tvn24.pl/tvn24-news-in-english/poland-bids-last-farewell-to-actress-barbara-krafftowna-5586252.

Chapter 11

211. "Stonington's New Club House," *Stonington (CT) Mirror*, 1909, November 26.
212. "Borough Liquor Cases," *Stonington (CT) Mirror*, January 29, 1901.
213. Ibid.
214. "Engels Acquitted," *Stonington (CT) Mirror*, February 5, 1910.
215. *Stonington (CT) Mirror*, October 24, 1912.
216. *Stonington (CT) Mirror*, December 4, 1913.
217. *Stonington (CT) Mirror*, November 5, 1914.
218. "Burnt to Death," *Stonington (CT) Mirror*, December 11, 1896.
219. Much of this account of William Loudon's life is drawn from his obituary: "William Loudon of Pawcatuck Dead at 84: Well-Known as Sidewalk-Builder and Land Developer," *Westerly (RI) Sun*, September 19, 1946.
220. U.S. Patent No. 738,689, September 8, 1903, https://patents.google.com/patent/US738689A/en?oq=US738689.
221. "Borough Places Raided and Fines Given," *Stonington (CT) Mirror and Mystic Journal*, November 20, 1925.

Acknowledgements

222. Glenn Thrush, "Anthony Bailey, Biographer with Restless Literary Spirit, Dies at 87," *New York Times*, May 26, 2020.

INDEX

ABOUT THE AUTHOR

Photo by Tim Martin.

Stuart Vyse is a psychologist and writer. He is a contributing editor at *Skeptical Inquirer* magazine, where he writes the Behavior & Belief column. He is the author of *Believing in Magic: The Psychology of Superstition* (Oxford, 2014), which won the William James Book Award of the American Psychological Association; *Going Broke: Why Americans (Still) Can't Hold On to Their Money* (Oxford, 2018); *Superstition: A Very Short Introduction* (Oxford, 2020); and most recently, *The Uses of Delusion: Why It's Not Always Rational to Be Rational* (Oxford, 2022). He has lived in Stonington, Connecticut, for over twenty years. All author proceeds from this book will be donated to the Stonington Historical Society (https://www.stoningtonhistory.org/).

Visit us at
www.historypress.com